CAMBRIDGE TEXTS IN THE
HISTORY OF POLITICAL THOUGHT

MACHIAVELLI
The Prince

CAMBRIDGE TEXTS IN THE HISTORY OF POLITICAL THOUGHT

Series editors
RAYMOND GEUSS
Lecturer in Philosophy, University of Cambridge

QUENTIN SKINNER
Regius Professor of Modern History in the University of Cambridge

Cambridge Texts in the History of Political Thought is now firmly established as the major student textbook series in political theory. It aims to make available to students all the most important texts in the history of western political thought, from ancient Greece to the early twentieth century. All the familiar classic texts will be included, but the series seeks at the same time to enlarge the conventional canon by incorporating an extensive range of less well-known works, many of them never before available in a modern English edition. Wherever possible, texts are published in complete and unabridged form, and translations are specially commissioned for the series. Each volume contains a critical introduction together with chronologies, biographical sketches, a guide to further reading and any necessary glossaries and textual apparatus. When completed the series will aim to offer an outline of the entire evolution of western political thought.

For a list of titles published in the series, please see end of book.

MACHIAVELLI

The Prince

EDITED BY

QUENTIN SKINNER

Regius Professor of Modern History in the University of Cambridge

AND

RUSSELL PRICE

Senior Lecturer in Politics,
University of Lancaster

CAMBRIDGE
UNIVERSITY PRESS

PUBLISHED BY THE PRESS SYNDICATE OF THE UNIVERSITY OF CAMBRIDGE
The Pitt Building, Trumpington Street, Cambridge, United Kingdom

CAMBRIDGE UNIVERSITY PRESS
The Edinburgh Building, Cambridge CB2 2RU, UK
40 West 20th Street, New York, NY 10011–4211, USA
477 Williamstown Road, Port Melbourne, VIC 3207, Australia
Ruiz de Alarcón 13, 28014 Madrid, Spain
Dock House, The Waterfront, Cape Town 8001, South Africa

http://www.cambridge.org

First published 1988
14th printing 2001

Printed in the United Kingdom at the University Press, Cambridge

British Library Cataloguing in Publication data
Machiavelli, Niccolò, *1469–1527*
Machiavelli: *The Prince*. –
(Cambridge texts in the history of political thought).
1. State. Theories – Early works
I. Title   II. Skinner, Quentin   III. Price, Russell
320.1'01

Library of Congress Cataloguing in Publication data
Machiavelli, Niccolò, 1469–1527.
[Principe. English]
Machiavelli: *The Prince* /
edited by Quentin Skinner and Russell Price.
p.   cm. –
(Cambridge texts in the history of political thought)
Translation from the Italian of: Il principe.
Bibliography.
Includes index.
ISBN 0 521 34240 6.   ISBN 0 521 34993 1 (pbk.)
1. Political science – Early works to 1800.   2. Political ethics.
I. Skinner, Quentin.   II. Price, Russell.   III. Title.
IV. Title: Prince.   V. Series.
JC143.M38 1988b
320.1 – dc 19   88–5048   CIP

ISBN 0 521 34240 6 hardback
ISBN 0 521 34993 1 paperback

Contents

Contents

Editors' note

The division of labour between us has been as follows. The Introduction was written by Quentin Skinner, who also compiled the Bibliographical Note and the list of Principal Events in Machiavelli's Life. But he is greatly indebted to Russell Price for the many helpful suggestions he made about each of these parts of the book. For commenting on drafts of the Introduction he would also like to express his warm thanks to Raymond Geuss, Susan James and Jeremy Mynott.

The translation is the work of Russell Price, who is also responsible for the annotations to the text, the Appendices, the Biographical Notes and the Indexes. But he in turn wishes to acknowledge his great debt to Quentin Skinner for checking the whole of the translation and for commenting on his other contributions to the book. He is also very grateful for the help received from several other friends, which has contributed greatly to improving the translation. He is especially indebted to Paolo L. Rossi, who checked most of it. He also wishes to thank Francesco Badolato, Luciano Cheles and Michael Oakeshott for commenting on some chapters, and for advice, as well as Bruna Isella and Rev. Giovanni Rulli, S. J., for advice on some points, and Harro Höpfl for help in correcting the proofs.

Introduction

Niccolò Machiavelli was born in Florence in 1469. He received his early education from a well-known teacher of Latin, Paolo da Ronciglione, and may subsequently have attended the University of Florence. After that, however, almost nothing is known about him until 1498. In the spring of that year the regime dominated by Savonarola fell from power in Florence. A new city government was elected, and Machiavelli was one of those who rose to prominence in the wake of the change. Although he appears to have held no previous public office, he suddenly found himself installed both as head of the second Chancery and as secretary to the main foreign relations committee of the republic, the so-called Ten of War.

Machiavelli served the Florentine republic for over fourteen years, during which he was sent on a number of diplomatic missions on behalf of the Ten. In the course of these embassies he wrote a large body of official reports, trying out many of the ideas he was later to develop in his political works. He also came into direct contact with many of the political leaders whose policies he subsequently analysed in the pages of *The Prince*, including Louis XII of France, Cesare Borgia, Pope Julius II and the Emperor Maximilian.

Machiavelli's public career came to an abrupt end in the summer of 1512. During the previous October the Pope had signed the Holy League with Ferdinand of Spain. Entering Italy in the spring of 1512, Ferdinand's troops first drove the French out of Milan. Then they turned against Florence, the traditional ally of the French. Faced with the sack of their city, the Florentines capitulated at the end of August. The Medici family, in exile since 1494, returned to its earlier position of controlling influence in the city, and soon afterwards the institutions of the republic were dissolved.

Machiavelli's own misfortunes began in November, when he was formally dismissed from his post in the Chancery. (Why he was suddenly removed, however, remains something of a mystery, especially as some of his friends survived the change of regime without apparent difficulty.) A second blow fell in February 1513, when he was accused of taking part in an abortive conspiracy against the new regime. At first he was imprisoned and tortured, but soon afterwards he was released and allowed to retire to his farm. From there, in December 1513, he wrote a famous letter to his friend Francesco Vettori about his new life. I have been making it bearable, he reports, by studying ancient history, and at the same time pondering the lessons to be gleaned from long years of government service. As a result, he says, 'I . . . have composed a little book *On Principalities*, in which I delve as deeply as I can into this subject' (p. 93). The little book is *The Prince*, which Machiavelli drafted – as this letter indicates – in the second half of 1513 and completed by the end of that year.

The Prince opens with the observation that all forms of dominion are either republics or principalities (Ch. I). But Machiavelli at once adds that he will concern himself exclusively with principalities, concentrating on the best methods of governing and holding on to them (Ch. II). His aim in doing so, as his opening Dedicatory Letter explains, is to show the Medici how to scale the heights of greatness. One of his hopes, he adds, is of course to win their favour by advising them on how this can be done. But his main aspiration – as he makes clear in the Exhortation to the Medici which brings *The Prince* to a close – is that if they follow his advice, the result will be to bring honour to their illustrious family and benefit to the people as a whole.

As Machiavelli points out at the start of Chapter XII, the first eleven chapters of his book form a unity. He begins by distinguishing three different types of principality, and proceeds to analyse the different methods of acquiring and maintaining them. First he considers hereditary principalities, but only to note that these pose few difficulties (Ch. II). Next he turns to what he calls mixed cases, those in which a ruler annexes a new possession to existing territories (Ch. III). This is where problems begin to arise, especially if the two principalities are in different areas and lack a shared language or system of laws.

Chapter III is given over to contrasting the Roman way of proceeding in such cases with the methods recently employed by Louis XII of France in attempting to hold on to his new possessions in Italy. The first and most effective policy, Machiavelli insists no less than three times, is for the ruler of such a composite principality to go and live in his new territories. Thereafter he must devote himself to undermining his stronger neighbours while protecting the weaker ones. The Romans always acted in this fashion, as a result of which they never lost control of new provinces. But Louis has done exactly the opposite, as a result of which he has just been hounded out of Milan for the second time.

Newly acquired territories will either be accustomed to living under a prince (Ch. IV), or else will be self-governing republics used to living 'in freedom' (Ch. V). Territories of the former type are relatively easy to hold, provided that the previous ruler was someone who exercised total political control. But conquered republics are very hard to maintain, for they always display 'greater vitality, more hatred, and a stronger desire for revenge' (p. 19). A new ruler must either destroy them completely, or else be sure to go and live there, while at the same time allowing their citizens as many as possible of their old laws.

Machiavelli next turns from rulers who gain control of new territories to the contrasting case of private citizens who become rulers for the first time. He considers five different ways in which this transition can be effected, arguing that the obstacles a new prince can expect to encounter will largely depend on the manner in which his principality was first obtained.

One method of becoming a prince is by *virtú* and the force of one's own arms (Ch. VI). Principalities are hard to acquire in this way, but easy to hold once acquired. A second method is to gain power – as Cesare Borgia did – by good fortune and the arms of others (Ch. VII). Such rulers attain their positions with ease, but hold on to them only with the greatest difficulty. A third way is to come to power by crime (Ch. VIII). Machiavelli offers as his main example Agathocles of Sicily, who seized control of Syracuse after butchering the entire senate. A fourth way is to be chosen by one's fellow-citizens (Ch. IX). Princes of this type generally find little difficulty in holding on to power, provided they are able to retain the goodwill of those who originally chose them. Finally, a fifth method of rising from the status of a private citizen to that of a ruler is to be elected pope (Ch. XI).

Machiavelli presents this classification in a self-consciously cool and abstract style. When he discusses the attainment of power by crime, he remarks that he will not enter into the merits of the case, since his examples 'should be enough for anyone who needs to imitate them' (p. 30). And when he ends by discussing the Papacy, he insists on treating that august institution – in a manner that must certainly have startled his original readers – as nothing more than one of the various principalities contending for power in Italy.

Nevertheless, there is something deceptive about Machiavelli's presentation of his case. He is careful to develop his typologies and put forward his precepts in wholly general terms. But the factors he chooses to emphasise suggest that, at several crucial points, what he is really thinking about is the situation in Florence.

This becomes evident as soon as we recall the position of the Medici at the moment when Machiavelli was writing *The Prince*. At the time of their reinstatement in 1512, the Medici had been living in exile for eighteen years. They had thus spent most of their lives as private citizens. Moreover, the city to which they returned had been a self-governing republic throughout the intervening period. Finally, they owed their reinstatement not to their own *virtù*, but to sheer good fortune combined with the foreign arms supplied by Ferdinand of Spain.

This is to say that the Medici found themselves in the predicament Machiavelli considers most dangerous of all for a new prince. He is very emphatic in Chapter VII about the problems encountered by those who suddenly come to power by luck or favour in combination with the force of foreign arms: 'like all other natural things that are born and grow rapidly, states that grow quickly cannot sufficiently develop their roots, trunks and branches, and will be destroyed by the first chill winds of adversity' (p. 23). He insists in Chapter V that these problems will be even graver if their principality was previously a republic. For in republics 'they do not forget, indeed cannot forget, their lost liberties' (p. 19). Beneath the surface generalities of Machiavelli's text, a highly specific note of warning – possibly even of *Schadenfreude* – is clearly audible.

A similar point can be made if we consider how the Medici conducted themselves in Florence during the years immediately after their return. Giuliano de' Medici, the man to whom Machiavelli originally dedicated *The Prince*, was at first sent to take control. But the head of the family, Pope Leo X, recalled him to Rome as early as April 1513.

Giuliano's nephew Lorenzo, to whom Machiavelli rededicated his book after Giuliano's death in 1516, was thereupon sent in his place. But he too spent little time in the direct supervision of the city's affairs. He was absent from September 1514 until May 1515, and again for much of the rest of that year; he was absent again from October 1516 until the spring of the following year, and he died less than two years after that.

Throughout the period when Machiavelli was writing and revising *The Prince*, the Medici were thus behaving in just the manner that Machiavelli felt to be the height of imprudence. As we have seen, Chapter III argues that Louis XII's failure to go and live in his newly conquered Italian territories was one of the main causes of his losing them so rapidly. Chapter V adds that, in the case of new possessions which have previously been republics, it is absolutely indispensable either to destroy them or else to go and settle in their territories. Once again, an undercurrent of specific warning and advice appears to lie beneath the surface generalities of Machiavelli's text.

At the start of Chapter XII Machiavelli announces a new theme. Having discussed the various types of principality, he now turns to the figure of the prince. Unless a new prince builds firm foundations he will always come to grief. But the main foundations of any government are good arms and the good laws that arise out of them. The first and most basic topic to be considered must therefore be the prince's methods of defence.

Taking up this question in Chapters XII to XIV, Machiavelli makes two fundamental points. The first is that no prince can be said to have good arms unless he raises his own troops. And in speaking of *arme proprie*, as he explains at the end of Chapter XIII, what Machiavelli means are armies 'composed of subjects or citizens or of one's dependents' (p. 51). This is one of Machiavelli's cardinal beliefs, and it underlies practically everything he says about the best means of gaining and holding power. Chapter VI had already warned that even the greatest *virtù* will never be sufficient to maintain a new ruler unless he can also defend himself without the help of others. Chapter VII had declared that the first task of those who win power by favour or fortune is – as Cesare Borgia had recognised – to raise their own troops. And in Chapter XI Machiavelli had sardonically added that, although we cannot enquire into the workings of the Papacy, since it is controlled by a higher power, we can certainly ask why it has grown so rapidly in stature of recent years. The answer, once again, is simply that the popes have 'made it great by the use of force' (p. 42).

Machiavelli's argument constitutes a frontal attack on the advice-books for princes published by a number of his contemporaries. Giovanni Pontano, for example, writing his treatise on *The Prince* in the 1490s, had affirmed that any ruler who is loved by his subjects will never need to maintain an army at all. Machiavelli never tires of insisting that, on the contrary, sheer force is indispensable to good government. He not only makes this the principal theme of these central chapters on military affairs; he also reverts to the same topic in the last three chapters of his book.

These closing chapters begin by considering the various rulers who have recently lost power in Italy (Ch. XXIV). In every case, Machiavelli stresses, their first and basic failing was their 'common military weakness' (p. 83). This makes it absurd for them to claim that they have been the victims of sheer ill-fortune. The power of *fortuna*, as the celebrated discussion in Chapter XXV goes on to explain, need never control more than half our actions. They have lost their positions in consequence of lacking the kind of *virtú* with which Fortune can alone be opposed, and in particular the kind of military *virtú* needed for the successful defence of one's territories. The final Exhortation to the Medici largely echoes the same refrain. 'If your illustrious family, then, wants to emulate those great men who saved their countries, it is essential above all else, as a sound basis for every campaign, to form an army composed of your own men' (pp. 89–90).

Machiavelli's argument is also directed against the prevailing conduct of warfare in Italy. With the increasing refinement of urban as well as courtly life, most princes had given up attempting to muster their own armies and turned to the employment of mercenary and auxiliary troops. Against this practice Machiavelli speaks out with intense vehemence. Mercenaries are 'useless and dangerous'; the ruin of Italy 'has been caused by nothing else than the reliance over so many years on mercenary armies' (p. 43). Borrowed auxiliaries are even worse; if they lose they ruin you, but if they win they leave you at the mercy of the foreign ruler to whom they owe their basic allegiance (Ch. XIII).

Machiavelli's other main contention about the prince's military duties forms the subject of Chapter XIV. A ruler must always think and act essentially as a warrior, and above all take command of his armies himself. This too constitutes a sharp break with the usual values of Renaissance advice-books aimed at princes and their followers. Consider, for example, Castiglione's *Book of the Courtier*, drafted a few years before *The Prince*. Castiglione argues that, even among those whose profession is arms, warlike attitudes must of course be set aside in time of peace in order to cultivate the arts and refinements of civilised life. Machiavelli grimly points to the consequences of adopting such an attitude: 'it is evident that if rulers concern themselves more with the refinements of life than with military matters, they lose power' (p. 52). A prince, he concludes, 'should have no other objective and no other concern, nor occupy himself with anything else except war and its methods and practices' (pp. 51–2).

Following this discussion of military affairs, Machiavelli announces at the start of Chapter XV that one further question still needs to be raised about the figure of the prince. How should he conduct himself towards others, especially his allies and his own subjects? Machiavelli's answer occupies him throughout Chapters XV to XXIII, after which he concludes (as we have seen) by reverting to the topic of defence. The intervening chapters undoubtedly represent the most sensational and 'Machiavellian' sections of his book.

He begins by noting that 'many people have written about this subject' (p. 54). It is clear that he partly has in mind the advice-books produced by such prominent humanists as Patrizi and Platina as well as Pontano, all of whom had published treatises entitled *The Prince* in the course of Machiavelli's own lifetime. As he subsequently indicates, however, he also has in mind a number of ancient treatises to which these contemporary writers owed their deepest intellectual debt. The most influential of these included Seneca's book of advice to Nero, *De clementia*, and above all Cicero's general treatise on moral duties, *De officiis*, whose precepts were frequently copied out by Renaissance moralists virtually word-for-word.

At the same time Machiavelli alerts us to the fact that his own analysis will involve him in repudiating this entire tradition of thought. 'I fear that I may be thought presumptuous, for what I have to say differs from the precepts offered by others, especially on this matter' (p. 54). The reason, he adds, is that he finds existing discussions somewhat unrealistic, and hopes to say something useful by attempting instead to 'consider what happens in fact' (p. 55).

The fact is that, whenever rulers are discussed, they are described as having a range of qualities for which they are either praised or blamed. Some are held to be generous, others miserly; some cruel, others humane; some untrustworthy, others faithful to their word – and so on in an extensive list of princely vices and virtues.

Turning to consider these qualities one by one, Machiavelli registers two rather different doubts. He first suggests that, although some of the attributes for which princes are praised are held to be good qualities, they only appear to be virtues. He first makes this point in connection with the supposed virtue of generosity, the subject of Chapter XVI. To gain a public reputation for being generous, a prince will have to consume all his resources in sumptuous display. So he will end up in the paradoxical position of having to load his subjects with additional taxes in order to sustain his reputation as a generous man. A prince who refuses to act in this way will at first be called a miser, but in course of time he will come to seem a man of truer generosity.

Machiavelli presents a similar paradox in Chapter XVII, the theme of which is the supposed vice of cruelty. Here he considers the behaviour of his fellow-Florentines in connection with the riots at Pistoia in 1501, a crisis he himself had been sent to investigate as secretary to the Ten of War. Wishing to avoid any accusation of cruelty, the Florentines had refused to punish the leaders of the factions involved. The result was that the disturbances turned into a general massacre. It would have been more genuinely merciful, Machiavelli insists, if the Florentines had instead made an example of the ringleaders at the outset, even though this would of course have led to accusations of cruelty.

Machiavelli's main doubt about the conventional virtues, however, is a different and far more radical one. Everyone will agree, Chapter XV concedes, that it would be most praiseworthy if princes could in fact possess the full range of qualities usually held to be good. But the conditions of human life are such that this is impossible: 'how men live is so different from how they should live that a ruler who does not do what is generally done, but persists in doing what ought to be done, will undermine his power rather than maintain it' (p. 54). It follows that a prince who wishes to maintain his position in a world where so many people are not good 'must be prepared to act immorally when this becomes necessary' (p. 55).

Machiavelli devotes his ensuing chapters to explaining what he means by being prepared to act immorally. His way of proceeding at this critical juncture is to offer a point-by-point refutation of the conventional wisdom which had largely been inspired by Seneca's and especially Cicero's treatises.

First he reverts to the virtue of generosity (Ch. XVI). Cicero had opened his discussion of this quality in *De officiis* by declaring that nothing more befits the nature of man (I, 14, 42). Machiavelli begins by saying that, even if generosity is the name of a virtue, it can nevertheless do you great harm. Cicero had gone on to argue that the least suspicion of miserliness or avarice ought always to be avoided (II, 17, 58; II, 18, 64). Machiavelli argues that a wise prince will never mind being called miserly; he will recognise that it is one of the vices without which he cannot hope to sustain his rule. Cicero had repeatedly argued that generosity, together with justice, are the virtues that above all cause us to love those who possess them (I, 17, 56). A reputation for generosity in a leader always wins the intense affection of the people, whereas everyone hates those who discourage generosity (II, 17, 56; II, 18, 63). Machiavelli insists that it is the practice of generosity, not its discouragement, which eventually brings a prince hatred and contempt. And he notes – confronting theory with practice as he frequently does in these chapters – that in modern times great things have been done only by those princes who have had the reputation of being miserly.

Next Machiavelli turns to the vice of cruelty (Ch. XVII). The classic analysis of this evil, Seneca's *De clementia*, had denounced cruelty as the characteristic vice of tyrants, and hence as the evil most of all to be avoided by true princes (I, 26, 1). Machiavelli retorts that a wise ruler will never mind being called cruel for any action which has the effect of keeping his subjects united and loyal. The accepted image of the true prince, one mainly derived from Seneca's famous account, had pictured such a ruler as someone who avoids cruelty even when it might be expedient to embrace it. But Machiavelli insists that it is simply impossible for a prince, and especially a new prince, to avoid incurring a reputation for cruelty if he wishes to maintain his government.

Later in the same chapter Machiavelli considers the related dispute which arises, as he says, when one asks whether it is better for a prince to be loved or feared. Here he alludes directly to *De officiis*, II, 7, 23–4, where Cicero had discussed the best means to establish and secure power over others. To banish fear and hold fast to love, Cicero had affirmed, offers the best means to maintain our influence over other people and our own safety at the same time. Machiavelli responds with a flat contradiction: 'it is difficult to achieve both and, if one of them has to be lacking, it is much safer to be feared than loved' (p. 59). Cicero had gone on to add that there is no power so great that it can hope to last if it is upheld by fear (II, 7, 25). Machiavelli replies that, because men are in general so deeply self-interested, they will break the bonds of love whenever they find it useful, whereas fear of punishment will always hold them effectively.

Finally, Machiavelli asks how far a prince should honour his word (Ch. XVIII). Cicero's *De officiis* had treated it as axiomatic that the keeping of promises represents the foundation of justice (I, 7, 23). It had thus become proverbial to say that, even when dealing with our enemies, we must always regard our word as our bond. Machiavelli retorts that a prudent ruler ought never to keep his word if this would be contrary to his interests. And he adds – confronting theory with practice yet again – that in recent times the only princes who have achieved great things have been those who have set little store by the keeping of promises.

As Machiavelli develops this critique of classical humanism, it becomes increasingly evident that it is underpinned by a darkly pessimistic view of human nature. Men can never be expected to keep faith, Machiavelli declares, nor to behave well in any other way, unless they are made to fear the consequences of behaving badly. This perception in turn controls his handling of a further issue often discussed in Renaissance advice-books for princes, that of how rulers should conduct themselves towards their counsellors and others occupying positions of influence in their government.

Cicero had provided a much-quoted description in *De officiis* of the qualities that make citizens worthy to occupy such positions of influence. They must be ready to devote themselves entirely to their country's interests, and must never seek power or wealth on their own behalf (I, 25, 86). Discussing the same subject in Chapter XXII, Machiavelli makes clear his scepticism about whether such counsellors are anywhere to be found. There is only one way, he argues, to keep your advisers honest and trustworthy. You must load them with so many honours and so much wealth that they come to depend on you completely. This alone ensures that they keep faith with you and avoid looking for even greater rewards elsewhere.

If the usual advice-books for princes contain so many dangerously idealised precepts, what positive advice can be offered to new princes of a more realistic and hence a more useful character? This is the question Machiavelli begins to address at the end of Chapter XVIII, and it occupies him for the remainder of this part of his book.

Machiavelli may be said to offer two main precepts which, he claims, will enable a new prince who follows them to rule with no less assurance than a well-established one. The first, which arises directly out of his critique of the mirror-for-princes literature, is initially put forward at the end of Chapter XVIII. It is good actually to possess all the qualities usually held to be admirable. And even if (or rather, especially if) you do not in fact possess them, it is absolutely essential that you should appear to do so. But if you wish to maintain your position, it is no less essential that you should be prepared to disregard the conventional virtues and 'be capable of entering upon the path of wrongdoing when this becomes necessary' (p. 62).

This doctrine embodies two further and especially pointed allusions to the usual humanist pieties. The first is contained in the suggestion that princes must always appear virtuous, and must therefore learn how to dissimulate. Cicero had sternly warned in *De officiis* against assuming that true glory can ever be gained by vain displays or hypocritical talk. All such pretences fall to the ground as quickly as fragile flowers, for nothing counterfeit possesses any lasting quality (II, 12, 43). Machiavelli satirises these earnest sentiments with obvious relish. The truth is, he insists, that 'men are so naive, and so much dominated by immediate needs, that a skilful deceiver always finds plenty of people who will let themselves be deceived' (p. 62).

Machiavelli's other and even more pointed satire is contained in his suggestion that rulers must cultivate two natures – a good one which they should follow when possible, and a bad one which they must be prepared to follow when this is dictated by necessity. Cicero had already observed in *De officiis* that there are two ways of gaining one's ends. One is by argument, the other by force; the first is proper to men, the second only to beasts (I, 11, 34). Sharpening the distinction, Cicero had added that beastly methods, encompassing the use of fraud as well as force, are completely unworthy of men. Force reduces us to the level of the lion, fraud to that of the fox, and both must be avoided at all costs (I, 13, 41).

Taking up Cicero's discussion almost word-for-word, Machiavelli begins by agreeing that there are indeed two ways of contending, either by laws or else by physical force. He also agrees that the former method is proper to men, the latter to beasts. Then he springs his trap: 'but because the former is often ineffective, one must have recourse to the latter' (p. 61). This means that a prince, being committed to beastly methods, ought to know which beasts to imitate. Turning Cicero on his head, Machiavelli puts forward his celebrated advice: a prince will do best if he learns to 'imitate both the fox and the lion' (p. 61).

Summarising this part of his argument, Machiavelli reiterates that wise princes are governed not by the requirements of the conventional virtues but rather by necessity. Specifically, they understand that it is often necessary to act contrary to the conventional virtues in order to maintain their government.

This point can also be expressed in a different way that brings out more effectively the radical character of Machiavelli's argument. As we have seen, when Machiavelli first considers in Chapter VI the range of qualities that enable a ruler to gain power and hold it with a minimum of difficulty, he uses the general term *virtù* to describe the qualities required. One way, therefore, of describing Machiavelli's ideal is to say that it embodies a new conception of how the crucial concept of *virtù* should be understood. A prince who knows how to maintain his government – and is therefore to be accounted a true *virtuoso* – will be 'prepared to vary his conduct as the winds of fortune and changing circumstances constrain him' (p. 62). To be a truly *virtuoso* prince is to be willing and able to do whatever is necessary for the preservation of one's government. So Machiavellian *virtù* consists in a willingness to follow the virtues when possible and an equal willingness to disregard them when necessary.

Machiavelli announces his other main precept at the start of Chapter XIX. At this point he simply draws upon an observation that would have been familiar to most of his original readers from Aristotle's *Politics*. Surveying the causes of revolution in Book V, Aristotle had concluded that monarchies, and especially new monarchies, usually collapse when their rulers come to be viewed either with hatred or with contempt (1312b). Machiavelli reiterates exactly the same argument. A new prince who wishes to maintain his state must 'avoid anything that will make him either hated or despised' (p. 63).

As Machiavelli stresses later in the same chapter, the same precept can also be expressed in a more positive way. A ruler who wishes to hold on to power must ensure above all that the whole populace, nobles and ordinary citizens alike, remain respectful and content with his government. As we have seen, Machiavelli had already argued in Chapter IX that, even when a prince is in some way chosen to rule, his only hope of securing his government will be to retain the goodwill of the people. He now makes that insight central to his argument. 'Well-ordered states and wise rulers have always been very careful not to exasperate the nobles and also to satisfy the people and keep them contented; this is one of the most important things for a ruler to do' (p. 66).

Machiavelli in turn applies this principle as a means of determining what should be said about two topical issues in Florentine politics. The first, taken up in Chapter XIX, concerns the danger of conspiracies. This was certainly a threat the Medici had good cause to fear. The Pazzi family had succeeded in assassinating Giuliano de' Medici in 1478, and Machiavelli himself had been arrested, as we have seen, in connection with a further plot in 1513. But the menace, Machiavelli declares, can easily be contained. Conspiracy is so dangerous that those who engage in it only do so if they think their action will be popular. It follows that the best shield a prince can have against conspiracy is simply to ensure that he never falls out of favour with the people.

The other topical issue Machiavelli considers is whether princes should guard their territories with fortresses. This forms the theme of Chapter XX, in the course of which Machiavelli notes that, although the Sforzas have built fortresses and the Florentines have used them to hold Pisa, the Duke of Urbino and the Bentivoglio in Bologna have both preferred to raze them to the ground. Again Machiavelli offers his own judgement in his briskest style. If you fear the hatred of your own subjects you must certainly build fortresses. But even this policy cannot in the end protect you against popular discontent. Hence 'the best fortress a ruler can have is not to be hated by the people' (p. 75).

For Machiavelli, accordingly, the principal question that remains is how to ensure that you do in fact retain the goodwill of the people and avoid incurring their hatred or contempt. Aristotle had laid it down in his *Politics* that rulers generally come to be hated as a result of confiscating the property of their subjects or violating the honour of their womenfolk (1311a–b). To this the Roman moralists had added that cruelty is another leading cause of hatred. As Seneca had put it in *De clementia*, cruelty always increases the number of a king's enemies and eventually makes him hated and loathed (I, 8, 7; I, 25, 3). It is striking that Machiavelli completely ignores this latter argument. But it is even more striking that, in offering his own opinion about how to avoid hatred, he simply reiterates what Aristotle had already said. It is not difficult, he argues in Chapter XIX, for a prince to avoid becoming hated; all he need do is ensure that he commits no outrages against the property or womenfolk of his subjects.

Turning finally to the question of how to avoid contempt, Machiavelli again gives his answer in the form of an implicit commentary on his classical authorities. In this case, however, he reverts to his more usual stance as critic, invoking but at the same time largely dissenting from traditional patterns of argument.

In one way Machiavelli thinks it easier to avoid contempt than earlier writers had supposed. Aristotle had thought of contempt as chiefly visited on rulers who lead a life of debauchery and drunkenness. He had therefore counselled rulers to behave with studied moderation in matters of personal and especially sexual morality (1314b). Cicero and his followers had underlined the same judgement in an even more puritanical style, stressing that a life of what Cicero calls 'decorum' and temperance is indispensable for anyone engaged in public affairs.

Machiavelli clearly regards these considerations as an irrelevance. Although he mentions lasciviousness as one of the qualities for which princes are blamed, he never takes up the suggestion that this is one of the failings that can actually endanger princely government. And when he discusses the range of vices that carry no such danger, the most he is prepared to say is that one should guard against them if one can, but that 'if one cannot bring oneself to do this, they can be indulged in with fewer misgivings' (p. 55). The classical ideal of self-control is dismissed with a shrug.

In another way, however, Machiavelli regards the avoidance of contempt as more difficult than had usually been supposed. This emerges most clearly from his handling of yet another standard topic in the literature of advice-books for princes, the topic of flatterers and how to avoid them. One familiar answer took the form of suggesting that the prince should make it clear that he wishes everyone to tell him the unvarnished truth at all times. He should therefore present himself – as Seneca had advised in *De clementia* – as a man of affability, easy of approach and openly accessible to all (I, 13, 4). Turning to this issue in Chapter XXIII, Machiavelli points to an obvious danger with this approach. If everyone feels free to tell the prince whatever they like at all times, he will very soon lose their respect and become an object of contempt.

How then is contempt to be avoided? Machiavelli gives part of his answer in criticising the image of the affable prince in Chapter XXIII. A prince ought not to allow anything like complete freedom of debate; he ought only to listen to a few advisers, and ought only to consult them on topics he himself wishes to hear discussed. But the main part of Machiavelli's answer seems to derive less from reflecting on the literature of advice-books than from observing the actual behaviour of contemporary rulers, especially the contrasting behaviour of the Emperor Maximilian and King Ferdinand of Spain. What makes princes appear contemptible, Chapter XIX declares, is seeming changeable, pusillanimous and irresolute. So to avoid contempt, Chapter XXI suggests, it is essential to avoid neutrality, a sure sign of weakmindedness. More positively, you must do what Septimius Severus did as Emperor of Rome and Ferdinand has done as King of Spain. You must undertake mighty schemes of a kind that keep the entire populace in a state of perpetual wonder and amazement.

Machiavelli largely presents his ideal of the *virtuoso* prince as a positive and creative force. Underlying his analysis, however, there is also a hint of Tacitean doubt. (It is perhaps significant that Tacitus is the one classical moralist approvingly cited for his wisdom in the course of *The Prince*.) Sometimes the ruler who is guided by necessity is pictured not as someone who uses his *virtú* to beat down the malice of Fortune, but simply as someone who successfully learns to adapt himself to political exigencies.

Machiavelli originally gave expression to this more sceptical outlook in a letter to his friend Giovan Soderini in 1506. Nature, he declares, 'produces different kinds of mind and temperament' by which we are all controlled. But times are varied and are subject to frequent change. So a man who wishes to enjoy good fortune will have to be 'shrewd enough to understand the times and circumstances' (p. 98). Writing *The Prince* seven years later, Machiavelli repeats these observations virtually word-for-word in his portrayal of Fortune in Chapter XXV. He begins by reaffirming that a prince can only hope to attain his ends if he manages to relate his ways of acting to the character of the times. But he now adds the blankly pessimistic suggestion that we can never hope to encounter anyone so prudent as to be able to adjust their behaviour in the appropriate way. The outcome is that, for all the magnificence of the rhetoric in the Exhortation that follows, Machiavelli ends on a fatalistic note. Since our circumstances vary, while our natures remain fixed, political success is simply a matter of having the good fortune to suit the spirit of the age.

Machiavelli is often described as a cynical writer, but this hardly seems an apt characterisation of *The Prince* as a whole. Consciously shocking though it often is, the work is passionately driven forward by a sense of what must realistically be said and done if political success is to be achieved. It is true, however, that a different and far more hollow tone is sounded towards the end. By concluding that political success may be nothing more than successful time-serving, Machiavelli takes leave of his readers on a genuinely cynical note.

Machiavelli undoubtedly hoped that *The Prince* would bring him to the favourable attention of the Medicean government. But in this he was disappointed. He was never entrusted with public office again, and spent the remaining fifteen years of his life as a man of letters. He first turned his attention to his *Discourses* on Livy, the work in which he developed his full-scale analysis of republican government. He then composed his treatise on *The Art of War*, his one work of statecraft to be printed during his own lifetime. Finally, he accepted a commission – ironically enough, from the Medici – to write his *Florentine Histories*, a task he completed some two years before his death in 1527.

Machiavelli's later political writings were all more leisurely and expansive than *The Prince*. But perhaps for that very reason, *The Prince* has always exercised the greatest hold over the imagination of succeeding generations. It was there that Machiavelli first presented, with matchless clarity and force, his basic assumption that rulers must always be prepared to do evil if good will come of it. In doing so he threw down a challenge which subsequent writers on statecraft have found it almost impossible to ignore.

Principal events in Machiavelli's life

1469 *May*: born (3rd) in Florence.

1481 *November*: begins to attend Paolo da Ronciglione's school.

Late 1480s Possibly attended lectures by Marcello Adriani at the University of Florence around this time.

1498 *June*: confirmed by Great Council as second chancellor of the Florentine republic.

July: elected secretary to the Ten of War.

November: mission to the ruler of Piombino, the first of a series of diplomatic missions undertaken by Machiavelli on behalf of the Ten.

1499 *July*: mission to Caterina Sforza-Riario.

1500 *July to December*: mission to court of Louis XII of France.

1501 Marries Marietta Corsini. (They eventually have six children.)

1502 *October*: mission to court of Cesare Borgia (Duke Valentino) at Imola.

December: follows Borgia to Cesena and Senigallia.

1503 *January*: returns from Borgia's court.

April: mission to Pandolfo Petrucci, ruler of Siena.

October to December: mission to papal court at Rome to report on election of Julius II.

1504   *January to February*: second mission to court of Louis XII.

      July: second mission to Pandolfo Petrucci.

1505   *December*: scheme for a revived Florentine militia, put forward by Machiavelli, provisionally accepted.

1506   *January*: helps to recruit for the militia in the Mugello, north of Florence.

      August to October; second mission to papal court; follows Julius II from Viterbo to Orvieto, Perugia, Urbino, Cesena and Imola.

      December: Great Council establishes a new committee, the Nine of the Militia, with Machiavelli as secretary.

1507   *December*: sent on mission to the Emperor Maximilian's court.

1508   *June*: returns from imperial court.

1510   *June to September*: third mission to court of Louis XII.

1511   *September*: fourth mission to court of Louis XII.

1512   *August*: Spanish troops attack Florentine territory and sack Prato.

      September: Florence surrenders; return of the Medici; dissolution of the republic.

      November: Machiavelli dismissed from the Chancery (7th) and sentenced (10th) to confinement within Florentine territory for a year.

1513   *February*: accused of taking part in anti-Medicean conspiracy; tried, tortured, imprisoned.

      March: released (11th) from prison.

      April: retires to his farm at Sant' Andrea in Percussina, 7 miles south of Florence.

      July (?) to December: writes draft of *Il Principe*.

c. 1515   Begins to frequent discussion-group presided over by Cosimo Rucellai in the Orti Oricellari, Florence. Dedicating his

Discorsi to Rucellai, Machiavelli implies that the book was written at Rucellai's behest and that it was discussed at these meetings.

1518   Writes *Mandragola*.

1518 or 1519   Completes *Discorsi*.

1520   Writes *Arte della guerra* and *La vita di Castruccio Castracani da Lucca*.

   November: receives commission from Cardinal Giulio de' Medici (later Pope Clement VII) to write the history of Florence.

1521   *Arte della guerra* published.

1525   *May*: visits Rome to present his completed *Istorie fiorentine* to Pope Clement VII.

1526   Revises and adds to *Mandragola*.

1527   *June*: dies (21st); buried (22nd) in Santa Croce, Florence.

1531   *Discorsi* published.

1532   *Il Principe* and *Istorie fiorentine* published.

Bibliographical note

Biography

The standard account is R. Ridolfi, *The Life of Niccolò Machiavelli*, trans. C. Grayson (London, 1963). On Machiavelli's entry into public life see N. Rubinstein, 'The Beginnings of Niccolò Machiavelli's Career in the Florentine Chancery', *Italian Studies* 11 (1956), pp. 72–91, and R. Black, 'Florentine Political Traditions and Machiavelli's Election to the Chancery', *Italian Studies* 40 (1985), pp. 1–16. For his conduct in office see F. Chiappelli, 'Machiavelli as Secretary', *Italian Quarterly* 14 (1970), pp. 27–44. For a highly readable narrative of his diplomatic missions see J. R. Hale, *Machiavelli and Renaissance Italy* (London, 1961). On his relations with the Rucellai circle see F. Gilbert, 'Bernardo Rucellai and the Orti Oricellari: A Study on the Origin of Modern Political Thought', in F. Gilbert, *History: Choice and Commitment* (Cambridge, Mass., 1977), pp. 215–46.

Intellectual background

For the most up-to-date survey of the intellectual life of the period see *The Cambridge History of Renaissance Philosophy*, ed. C. Schmitt, E. Kessler and Q. Skinner (Cambridge, 1988). On the development of Italian humanism, the essays collected in P. O. Kristeller, *Renaissance Thought*, 2 vols. (New York, 1961–5) are indispensable. For an outline of Renaissance political theory see Q. Skinner, *The Foundations of Modern Political Thought*, 2 vols. (Cambridge, 1978). The background of Florentine political theory is classically surveyed in H. Baron, *The Crisis of the Early Italian Renaissance* (revised edn, Princeton, 1966).

Political background

On the growth of Medicean power see N. Rubinstein, *The Government of Florence under the Medici 1434–1494* (Oxford, 1966). On the late fifteenth century see D. Weinstein, *Savonarola and Florence* (Princeton, 1970), and N. Rubinstein, 'Politics and Constitution in Florence at the End of the Fifteenth Century', in *Italian Renaissance Studies*, ed. E. F. Jacob (London, 1960), pp. 148–83. For the period when Machiavelli held public office see H. C. Butters, *Governors and Government in Early Sixteenth-Century Florence, 1502–1519* (Oxford, 1985). On the return of the Medici see J. N. Stephens, *The Fall of the Florentine Republic 1512–1530* (Oxford, 1983). For an outline of the whole story see J. R. Hale, *Florence and the Medici* (London, 1977).

General studies of *The Prince*

The relevant sections in F. Gilbert, *Machiavelli and Guicciardini* (revised edn, New York, 1984) are outstanding. So too the chapter on *The Prince* in J. G. A. Pocock, *The Machiavellian Moment* (Princeton, 1975). I. Berlin, 'The Originality of Machiavelli', in *Against the Current*, ed. H. Hardy (London, 1979), pp. 25–79, analyses Machiavelli's political morality. For a strongly contrasting viewpoint see L. Strauss, *Thoughts on Machiavelli* (Glencoe, Ill., 1958). For a readable outline (very critical of Machiavelli) see S. Anglo, *Machiavelli: A Dissection* (London, 1969). For a brief survey of Machiavelli's main works see Q. Skinner, *Machiavelli* (revised edn, Oxford, 1985). For a challenging recent reading of *The Prince*, focusing on Machiavelli's alleged inconsistencies, see M. McCanless, *The Discourse of Il Principe* (Malibu, 1983).

Specific aspects of *The Prince*

On the circumstances of its composition see F. Chabod, *Machiavelli and the Renaissance* (London, 1958). On its relationship with Machiavelli's other works see H. Baron, 'Machiavelli: The Republican Citizen and the Author of *The Prince*', *English Historical Review* 76 (1961), pp. 217–53. On its relationship with the 'mirror-for-princes' literature see F. Gilbert, 'The Humanist Concept of the Prince and *The Prince* of Machiavelli', in *History: Choice and Commitment*, pp. 91–114, and A. Gilbert, *Machiavelli's 'Prince' and its Forerunners* (Durham, N. C.,

1938). On its satirical relationship with classical humanism see M. Colish, 'Cicero's *De Officiis* and Machiavelli's *Prince*', *Sixteenth Century Journal*, 9 (1978), pp. 81–94.

Some leading concepts in *The Prince*

On *ambizione* see R. Price, '*Ambizione* in Machiavelli's Thought', *History of Political Thought* 3 (1982), pp. 382–445. On *fortuna*, J. Macek, '"La Fortuna" chez Machiavel', *Le Moyen Age*, 77 (1971), pp. 305–28, 493–524, T. Flanagan, 'The Concept of *Fortuna* in Machiavelli', in *The Political Calculus* ed. A. Parel (Toronto, 1972), pp. 127–56, and H. Pitkin, *Fortune is a Woman* (Berkeley, 1984). On *gloria*, R. Price, 'The Theme of *Gloria* in Machiavelli', *Renaissance Quarterly* 30 (1977), pp. 588–631. On *libertà*, M. Colish, 'The Idea of Liberty in Machiavelli', *Journal of the History of Ideas*, 32 (1971), pp. 323–50. On *ordini*, J. H. Whitfield, 'On Machiavelli's Use of *Ordini*', in *Discourses on Machiavelli* (Cambridge, 1969), pp. 141–62. On *lo stato*, J. H. Hexter, '*Il Principe* and *lo stato*', in *The Vision of Politics on the Eve of the Reformation* (London, 1973), pp. 150–78. On *virtú*, J. H. Whitfield, 'The Anatomy of Virtue', in *Machiavelli* (Oxford, 1947), pp. 92–105, N. Wood, 'Machiavelli's Concept of *Virtú* Reconsidered', *Political Studies* 15 (1967), pp. 159–72, J. H. Hexter, 'The Loom of Language and the Fabric of Imperatives: The Case of *Il Principe* and *Utopia*', in *The Vision of Politics*, pp. 179–203, and R. Price, 'The Senses of *Virtú* in Machiavelli', *European Studies Review* 3 (1973), pp. 315–45.

Translator's note

I have tried to provide a translation that is both accurate and readable. To make it more readable, I have not hesitated to break up some of Machiavelli's longer sentences; and I have divided the text into more paragraphs than is customary (the early manuscripts and the first edition have no paragraphs) in order to expose the main sections of the various chapters.

For the most part, Machiavelli expounded lucidly the themes and topics that concerned him in *The Prince*. His prose is usually straightforward, and he is not a verbose writer. (When he does use together two words that apparently have the same meaning, it will be found on inspection that they bear slightly different senses.) Moreover, 'rhetorical' passages are rarer in Machiavelli's works than in those of many Italian writers. He emphasises in the 'Dedicatory letter' his avoidance of rhetorical devices, saying that he has refrained from embellishing his book with 'rounded periods, with high-sounding words or fine phrases'. The passionate final chapter of *The Prince*, which is full of Biblical and other images, is markedly different in tone and style from the other chapters.

Nevertheless, Machiavelli is not an easy writer to translate. First, his word order is sometimes peculiar, and his writing is not always grammatical: the more pedantic commentators criticise him for writing some incoherent sentences (for 'anacolutha'); he sometimes changes the grammatical subject in mid-sentence, and he composes many sentences in which the subject is unexpressed, and has to be inferred from the sense. Secondly, in avoiding verbosity, Machiavelli sometimes goes to the opposite extreme: there are some very elliptical phrases and sentences that do not yield their meaning readily. Thirdly, he appears to have occasionally expressed his views with deliberate vagueness or ambiguity: thus, his opinions on the moral aspects of ruling and other political activities (see especially Chs. XV–XVIII) are notably less clear than those on the value of mercenaries, auxiliaries and citizen militias (Chs. XII–XIII). Fourthly, he does not usually define the terms he uses; this is especially true of the more abstract terms. *Prudenzia* ('prudence') is the only abstract term defined in *The Prince* (p. 79), if one excludes the negative characterisation of *virtú* on p. 31. Finally, as Lisio observed long ago, Machiavelli had a predilection for words that have several senses and various overtones.

Thus, *respetto* combines the senses of 'respect' and 'fear', sometimes with overtones of 'hesitation', 'reluctance' or 'caution': when one has *respetto* for another ruler's power one will hesitate to oppose or attack him. Again, *reverire* combines the senses of 'to fear' and 'to respect'; when a ruler or general is described as *reverito*, it means that he is regarded by others with a 'respectful fear'. The noun *sospetto* means 'fear' as well as 'suspicion', and sometimes it combines both of these senses (see p. 52). Sometimes *dubitare* signifies 'to doubt' or even 'to wonder' (see p. 33) but more often it means 'to fear', with overtones of 'doubt' or 'uncertainty'. Again, *industria* sometimes denotes 'industry' or 'persistence', but usually (as in the phrase *con ogni industria*) a preparedness to resort to any means to achieve one's ends is implied; sometimes (as when it is opposed to *forza*, 'force') it denotes 'craftiness' or 'guile' (p. 14); and in one passage (p. 8) it is used as a synonym of *virtú*, and denotes 'ability'. Moreover, *industria* also denotes an 'occupation' (e.g., p. 38). *Reputazione* usually means 'reputation' or 'prestige', but occasionally it denotes primarily 'power', 'position' or 'standing', which is of course always accompanied by a certain 'reputation'. What Louis XII regained after conquering Lombardy was not so much a 'reputation' as a 'position of power and influence', with a consequent increase of his 'reputation' (see p. 12).

These examples illustrate the point sufficiently. But there are other terms that have several senses and, like *industria* and *reputazione*, they denote key-ideas in *The Prince*: e.g., *virtú, fortuna, stato, ordini, spegnere, libertà, amico* and *amicizia*. Because of their importance, they are discussed fairly fully in Appendix B.

There are three other topics that should be mentioned here. Machiavelli uses many images in *The Prince*. Most of these similes and metaphors are undoubtedly very effective, and contribute notably to making *The Prince* the literary classic that it is. But there are some images that are either less effective or are difficult to render satisfactorily in another language. This applies particularly to some of the metaphors. However, I have concluded that, especially in a translation designed primarily for students, I should try to translate as many of these metaphors as possible, even if they do not always read very well in English.

Italian writers tend to overstate their case rather than understate it, and Machiavelli is no exception. Like some other translators, I have occasionally toned down his over-emphatic statements. For example, in Chapter X, Machiavelli says that a ruler whose city is well fortified, and who does not incur hatred, 'cannot be *assaltato*'; I have rendered this 'is safe from attack', because Machiavelli then says that if it should happen that another ruler launches an attack it will be unsuccessful. Again, in Chapter XXV, Machiavelli discusses Julius II; if he had acted very prudently, the French king would have advanced 'a thousand' excuses, and the others 'a thousand' fears. I have rendered *mille* as 'countless'. And, in Chapter XVII, Machiavelli discusses Hannibal and speaks of *infinite sua virtú*. I have usually rendered *infiniti* as 'countless'; but although the word may be used (with perhaps permissable exaggeration) to qualify 'victories' or 'defeats', I think it is definitely inappropriate here: accordingly, I have rendered this phrase as 'his many good qualities' (p. 60).

The text of *Il Principe* is in Italian, but some Latin is also used. In the early manuscripts the chapter-titles are in Latin. The Italian chapter-titles in the first edition were not, it seems, written by Machiavelli. Where there are significant differences between the Latin and Italian versions (as in Chs. VII and XIX) I have followed the version that seems most suited to the contents. Moreover, scattered throughout the work are various Latin words and phrases, such as *tamen*, *etiam* and *iure hereditario*. If Machiavelli had revised the book for publication, he might well have put the chapter-titles in Italian; in his other major works the chapter-titles are all in Italian, and very few Latin words or phrases occur in them (though the *Discourses* contains numerous quotations from Livy). Finally there are a few quotations from Livy, Virgil, Tacitus and Justinus. They are usually inaccurate, probably because quoted from memory. (Translations of these passages are given in the notes.)

The title itself is in Latin in the early manuscripts: *De principatibus*. And this is how Machiavelli refers to it in his letter to Vettori in 1513 (see p. 93); however, in the *Discourses* it is called a treatise *de Principati* (II, 1), and *De Principe* (III, 42).

NOTE ON THE TEXT

I have used the text edited by Sergio Bertelli, and published by Feltrinelli (Milan) in 1960; Bertelli's text (which is generally considered the most accurate) is based on that of Federico Chabod (1944, 2nd edn). But I have also taken account of Giuseppe Lisio's critical edition (1899), of Mario Casella's edition (1929), and of the various early manuscripts (Machiavelli's MS has not survived).

R.P.

November 1987

I have taken advantage of the reprinting of *The Prince* to make some corrections: the most important are on pp. xxxii, xxxiv, 13 note e, 41, 50, 58 note d, 89 note c and 108.

R.P.

May 1989

Northern and central Italy, c. 1500

The Prince

DEDICATORY LETTER

Niccolò Machiavelli to His Magnificence
Lorenzo de' Medici[a]

Those who wish to be viewed with favour by a ruler usually approach him with things from among their possessions that are very dear to them, or with things that they expect will please him. Hence, it often happens that they are presented with horses, weapons, a cloth of gold, precious stones and similar ornaments, which are worthy of their exalted position. Wishing myself to offer Your Magnificence some token of my devotion to you, I have not found among my belongings anything that I hold more dear or valuable than my knowledge of the conduct of great men, learned through long experience of modern affairs and continual study of ancient history: I have reflected on and examined these matters with great care, and have summarised them in a small volume, which I proffer to Your Magnificence.

And although I consider this work unworthy to be presented to Your Magnificence, I trust very much that your humanity will lead you to accept it, since it is not in my power to offer you a greater gift than one which in a very short time will enable you to understand all that I have learned in so many years, and with much difficulty and danger. I have not embellished this work by filling it with rounded periods, with high-sounding words or fine phrases, or with any of the other beguiling artifices of apparent beauty which most writers employ to describe and embellish their subject-matter; for my wish is that, if it is to be honoured at all, only its originality and the importance of the subject should make it acceptable.

[a Not Lorenzo the Magnificent, but the son of Piero de' Medici, and nephew of Pope Leo X.]

3

I hope it will not be considered presumptuous for a man of very low and humble condition to dare to discuss princely government, and to lay down rules about it. For those who draw maps place themselves on low ground, in order to understand the character of the mountains and other high points, and climb higher in order to understand the character of the plains. Likewise, one needs to be a ruler to understand properly the character of the people, and to be a man of the people to understand properly the character of rulers.

May Your Magnificence, then, accept this little gift in the spirit in which I am sending it; if it is read and pondered diligently, my deep wish will be revealed, namely, that you should achieve that greatness which propitious circumstances and your fine qualities promise. And if Your Magnificence, from the heights of your exalted position, should sometimes deign to glance down towards these lowly places, you will see how much I am unjustly oppressed by great and cruel misfortune.

CHAPTER I

The different kinds of principality and how they are acquired[a]

All the states, all the dominions that have held sway over men, have been either republics or principalities. Principalities are either hereditary (their rulers having been for a long time from the same family) or they are new. The new ones are either completely new (as was Milan to Francesco Sforza)[b] or they are like limbs joined to the hereditary state of the ruler who annexes them (as is the Kingdom of Naples to the King of Spain).[c] States thus acquired are either used to living under a prince or used to being free;[d] and they are acquired either with the arms of others or with one's own, either through luck or favour or else through ability.[e]

[a] This chapter summarises the topics discussed later, esp. in Chs. II–XI.]
[b] Sforza became Duke of Milan in 1450, putting an end to the short-lived Ambrosian republic, which arose after Filippo Maria Visconti's death in 1447.]
[c] Ferdinand the Catholic.]   [d] I.e., are republics.]
[e] This is the first instance of the antithesis between *fortuna* and *virtú*, which is so conspicuous in M.'s works. See esp. Chs. VI–IX.]

5

Chapter ii

Hereditary principalities

I shall not discuss republics, because I have previously treated them at length.[a] I shall consider only principalities, and shall weave together the warps mentioned above, examining how principalities can be governed and maintained.

I say, then, that states which are hereditary, and accustomed to the rule of those belonging to the present ruler's family, are very much less difficult to hold than new states, because it is sufficient not to change the established order, and to deal with any untoward events that may occur; so that, if such a ruler is no more than ordinarily diligent and competent, his government will always be secure, unless some unusually strong force should remove him. And even if that happens, whenever the conqueror encounters difficulties, the former ruler can re-establish himself.

To cite an Italian example: the Duke of Ferrara[b] resisted the assaults of the Venetians in 1484, as well as those of Pope Julius in 1510, just because his family was very well established in that state. For a natural ruler has fewer reasons and less need to harm others. Consequently, men will be better disposed towards him; and if he is not hated for unusually vicious conduct,[c] it is not surprising that he should be regarded with affection by his subjects. Moreover, the length and continuity of his family's rule extinguishes the memories of the causes of innovations:[d] for any change always leaves a toothing-stone for further building.

Chapter iii

Mixed principalities

However, it is in new principalities that there are real difficulties. First, if the principality is not completely new but is like a limb that is joined to

[a] This is probably an allusion to the *Discourses*, or perhaps to Bk I of that work. But it may well be a later interpolation.]
[b] Here M. conflates two Dukes of Ferrara, Ercole I and Alfonso I d'Este. See p. 123.]
[c] E.g., taking property or womenfolk belonging to others: see pp. 59, 63–4.]
[d] This sentence is not entirely clear; for Montanari, *le memorie e le cagioni* is an instance of hendiadys, and means 'the memory of the causes'.]

another principality (which taken together may almost be called a mixed principality), its mutability arises first from a very natural problem, which is to be found in all new principalities. This is that men are very ready to change their ruler when they believe that they can better their condition, and this belief leads them to take up arms against him. But they are mistaken, because they later realise through hard experience that they have made their condition worse. This arises from another natural and normal constraint, which is that anyone who becomes a new ruler is always forced to injure his new subjects, both through his troops and countless other injuries that are involved in conquering a state. The outcome is that you make enemies of all those whom you have injured in annexing a principality, yet you cannot retain the friendship of those who have helped you to become ruler, because you cannot satisfy them in the ways that they expect. Nor can you use strong medicine against them, since you have obligations to them. For even if one possesses very strong armies, the goodwill of the inhabitants is always necessary in the early stages of annexing a country.

These were the reasons why Louis XII of France quickly annexed Milan,[a] and just as quickly lost it;[b] and Ludovico's own troops were sufficiently powerful to deprive him of it the first time. For when the people who had opened the gates to Louis found that they did not receive the benefits they had expected, they could not endure the oppressive rule of the new master.[c]

It is certainly true that, after a country that has rebelled has been reconquered a second time, it is less likely to be lost, since the ruler, because of the rebellion, will be more ruthless in consolidating his power, in punishing the guilty, unmasking suspects, and remedying weaknesses in his government. Thus, a[d] Duke Ludovico creating a disturbance on the borders was enough to cause the King of France to lose Milan the first time. But to lose it a second time, it was necessary to have all the powers acting against him,[e] and for his armies to be defeated or driven out of Italy. This happened for the reasons mentioned above.

[a Sept. 1499.]
[b Ludovico Sforza returned to Milan on 5 Feb. 1500, but he lost it in April 1500.]
[c See p. 84.]
[d *uno*: the indefinite article expresses M.'s contempt for Ludovico Sforza.]
[e In April 1512, after the battle of Ravenna, in which the French were opposed by the army of the Holy League; Louis had retaken Milan in April 1500, after the battle of Novara.]

Nevertheless, he did lose Milan twice. The general reasons for the first loss have been discussed; it remains now to discuss the reasons for the second, and to consider what solutions were available to him, and what someone in his position might do, in order to maintain better than the King of France did the territory annexed.

I say, then, that the territories a conqueror annexes and joins to his own well-established state are either in the same country,[a] with the same language, or they are not. If they are, it is extremely easy to hold them, especially if they are not used to governing themselves.[b] To hold them securely, it is enough to wipe out the family of the ruler who held sway over them, because as far as other things are concerned, the inhabitants will continue to live quietly, provided their old way of life is maintained and there is no difference in customs. This has happened with Burgundy, Brittany, Gascony and Normandy, which have been joined to France for a long time.[c] Although there are some linguistic differences, nevertheless their way of life is similar, so no difficulties have arisen. Anyone who annexes such countries, and is determined to hold them, must follow two policies: the first is to wipe out their old ruling families; the second is not to change their laws or impose new taxes. Then the old principality and the new territory will very soon become a single body politic.

But considerable problems arise if territories are annexed in a country that differs in language, customs and institutions, and great good luck and great ability are needed to hold them. One of the best and most effective solutions is for the conqueror to go and live there.[d] This makes the possession more secure and more permanent. This is what the Turks did in Greece:[e] all the other measures taken by them to hold that country would not have sufficed, if they had not instituted direct rule. For if one does do that, troubles can be detected when they are just beginning and effective measures can be taken quickly. But if one does not, the troubles are encountered when they have grown, and nothing can be done about them. Moreover, under direct rule, the

---

[a *provincia*: it denotes any area that is larger than a 'city' or 'city-state' (*città*). See p. 103.]
[b *vivere liberi*: see p. 109.]
[c Normandy in 1204, Gascony in 1453, Burgundy in 1477, Brittany in 1491.]
[d I.e., to institute direct rule.]
[e 'Greece': M. meant the whole Balkan peninsula, which was subjected to Turkish invasions during the fifteenth century. The statement that the Turks lived in that state (or ruled it directly) refers to the fact that, after 1453, Constantinople became the capital of the new state.]

country will not be exploited by your officials; the subjects will be content if they have direct access to the ruler. Consequently, they will have more reason to be devoted to him if they intend to behave well, and to fear him if they do not. Any foreigners with designs on that state will proceed very carefully. Hence, if the state is ruled directly, it is very unlikely indeed to be lost.

The other very good solution is to establish colonies in a few places, which become, as it were, fetters for the conquered territory. If this is not done, it will be necessary to hold it by means of large military forces. Colonies involve little expense; and so at little or no cost, one establishes and maintains them. The only people injured are those who lose their fields and homes, which are given to the new settlers; but only a few inhabitants are affected in this way. Moreover, those whom he injures can never harm him, because they are poor and scattered. All the other inhabitants remain unharmed, and should therefore be reassured, and will be afraid of causing trouble, for fear that they will be dispossessed, like the others. I conclude that these colonies are not expensive, are more loyal, and harm fewer people; and those that are harmed cannot injure you because, as I said, they are scattered and poor.

It should be observed here that men should either be caressed or crushed; because they can avenge slight injuries, but not those that are very severe. Hence, any injury done to a man must be such that there is no need to fear his revenge.[a]

However, if military forces are sent instead of colonists, this is much more expensive, because all the revenue of the region will be consumed for its security. The outcome is that the territory gained results in loss to him; and it is much more injurious, because it harms the whole of that region when his troops move round the country. Everyone suffers this nuisance, and becomes hostile to the ruler. And they are dangerous enemies because, although defeated, they remain in their own homes. From every point of view, then, this military solution is misguided, whereas establishing colonies is extremely effective.

Again, as I have said, anyone who rules a foreign country should take the initiative in becoming a protector of the neighbouring minor powers and contrive to weaken those who are powerful within the country itself. He should also take precautions against the possibility

[a Cf. *Disc.* II, 23.]

9

that some foreign ruler as powerful as himself may seek to invade the country when circumstances are favourable. Such invaders are always helped by malcontents within the country, who are moved either by their own overweening ambition or by fear,[a] as happened in Greece, where the Aetolians were responsible for the invasion by the Romans. And in every country that the Romans attacked, some of the inhabitants aided their invasion. What usually happens is that, as soon as a strong invader attacks a country, all the less powerful men[b] rally to him, because they are enviously hostile to the ruler who has held sway over them. The invader has no trouble in winning over these less powerful men, since they will all be disposed to support the new power he has acquired. He needs only to be careful that they do not acquire too much military power and influence. And using his own forces, and with their consent, he can easily put down those who are powerful, thus gaining complete control of that country. A ruler who does not act in this way will soon lose what he has gained and, even while he does hold it, he will be beset by countless difficulties and troubles.

The Romans followed these policies very well in the countries they conquered. They established colonies, they had friendly relations with the less powerful (though without increasing their influence), they put down the powerful, and they ensured that strong foreign powers did not acquire influence in them.

I shall cite only Greece as an example. The Romans established friendly relations with the Achaeans and the Aetolians;[c] the Macedonian Kingdom was put down;[d] Antiochus was driven out;[e] they never permitted the Achaeans and the Aetolians to augment their power, despite the good offices rendered by them; Philip[f] sought to be accepted as their ally, but they would not permit any revival of his power; and even the might of Antiochus could not constrain them to let him hold any dominions in that country.

The Romans acted in these circumstances as all wise rulers should: for they have to deal not only with existing troubles, but with troubles

[a Fear of the ruler.]
[b Those who have *some* influence or power, not the masses.]
[c They were the 'less powerful' ones (*minor potenti*) in Greece.]
[d Philip V of Macedon was decisively defeated by Flaminius at Cynoscephalae in 197 B.C.]
[e Antiochus III, King of Syria, defeated by the Romans at Thermopylae in 191 B.C., and again at Magnesia in 190.]
[f Philip V of Macedon.]

that are likely to develop, and have to use every means to overcome them. For if the first signs of trouble are perceived, it is easy to find a solution; but if one lets trouble develop, the medicine will be too late, because the malady will have become incurable. And what physicians say about consumptive diseases is also true of this matter, namely, that at the beginning of the illness, it is easy to treat but difficult to diagnose but, if it has not been diagnosed and treated at an early stage, as time passes it becomes easy to diagnose but difficult to treat. This also happens in affairs of state; for if one recognises political problems early (which only a shrewd and far-seeing man can do),[a] they may be resolved quickly, but if they are not recognised, and left to develop so that everyone recognises them, there is no longer any remedy.

The Romans, therefore, because they perceived troubles when they were merely brewing, were always able to overcome them. They never allowed them to develop in order to avoid fighting a war, for they knew that wars cannot really be avoided but are merely postponed to the advantage of others. This was why they wanted to wage war against Philip and Antiochus in Greece, so that they could avoid having to fight them in Italy; it was possible for them to have avoided fighting both of them in Greece, but they were resolved not to. Moreover, the Romans never accepted a maxim heard every day on the lips of our own sages, to seek to benefit from temporising. They preferred to enjoy the benefits that derived from their own strength and prudence; because time brings all things with it, and can produce benefits as well as evils, evils as well as benefits.

However, let us return to the King of France, and examine whether he followed any of the policies I have advocated. I shall discuss Louis, not Charles;[b] since he held possessions in Italy for a longer period,[c] his conduct can be better studied. You will see that he did the opposite of what should be done in order to hold territory that is acquired in a foreign country.

King Louis's invasion of Italy was aided by the ambitious schemes of the Venetians, who wanted to gain half of Lombardy through that

[a In *Ist. fior.* VII, 5, M. remarks that Cosimo de' Medici ruled a difficult state 'for thirty-one years: because he was very prudent he recognised troubles when they were only brewing, and therefore had time to prevent them growing or to protect himself so that they would not harm him when they had grown'.]

[b Louis XII and Charles VIII.]

[c Louis maintained power in Italy from 1499 to 1512, whereas Charles was in Italy only between Aug. 1494 and July 1495.]

invasion.[a] I do not wish to criticise the policy adopted by the King: since he wanted to gain a foothold in Italy, and did not have any allies in this country (rather he found every gate closed to him, because of the conduct of Charles),[b] he was forced to make whatever alliances he could. And this good policy of his would have been successful, if he had not committed other errors. When he had conquered Lombardy, then, the King at once regained the power and prestige that had been lost by Charles. Genoa surrendered,[c] the Florentines became his allies; the Marquis of Mantua, the Duke of Ferrara, Bentivoglio, the Countess of Forlì, the rulers of Faenza, Pesaro, Rimini, Camerino, Piombino,[d] and the people of Lucca, Pisa and Siena: all of them moved to ally themselves with him. At this point, the Venetians were able to understand the rashness of their policy: in order to gain a couple of possessions in Lombardy, they had enabled the King to become master of a third[e] of Italy.

Everyone will realise how easily the King could have maintained his standing in Italy if he had followed the above-mentioned rules, and had maintained and protected all those allies of his who, because there were many of them, and they were weak and fearful (some of the power of the Church, some of the Venetians), were forced to remain allied to him. And with their help he could easily have dealt effectively with the remaining greater powers.

But no sooner was Louis in Milan than he began to follow the opposite policy, by helping Pope Alexander[f] to conquer the Romagna. Furthermore, he did not realise that this decision weakened him (because it alienated his allies and those who had thrown themselves in his lap)[g] and aggrandised the Church, for it added much temporal power to the spiritual power, from which it derives so much authority. After he had made his first blunder, he was forced to follow it up, so that, to put a stop to Alexander's ambitions, and to ensure that he did

[a] By the Treaty of Blois (April 1499), Louis promised the Ghiara d'Adda and Cremona to the Venetians.]

[b] Venice, Milan, Florence, Naples, Mantua, Spain and the Empire were all allied against Charles at the battle of Fornovo (6 July 1495).]

[c] In 1499; the French were driven out for the first time in 1507.]

[d] Respectively, Gian Francesco Gonzaga, Ercole I d'Este, Giovanni Bentivoglio, ruler of Bologna, Caterina Sforza Riario, Astorre Manfredi, Giovanni Sforza, Pandolfo Malatesta, Giulio Cesare da Varano, Iacopo IV Appiani.]

[e] Some texts have 'two-thirds', but this is not plausible.]

[f] In fact this was undertaken by Cesare Borgia (encouraged by Alexander). See p. 119.]

[g] I.e., who had rallied to him.]

not become master of Tuscany,[a] Louis was himself compelled to invade Italy.[b] It was not enough for him to have increased the power of the Church, and alienated his allies; because he coveted the Kingdom of Naples, he divided it with the King of Spain.[c] And whereas previously Louis had been arbiter of Italy, he now brought in a partner, so giving the ambitious men of that country and those who were discontented with him someone to turn to for help. Whereas he could have left in that Kingdom a tributary king, Louis removed him[d] and established there someone who could drive him out.

Wanting to annex territory is indeed very natural and normal, and when capable men undertake it, they are always praised or, at least, not criticised. But if men who are not capable of achieving it are bent on undertaking it at all costs, this is a blunder that deserves censure.

Hence, if the King of France could have attacked the Kingdom of Naples with his own troops, he should have done it; if he could not, he should not have tried to share it. And if sharing Lombardy with the Venetians deserves to be excused, because it enabled him to gain a foothold in Italy, this other sharing deserves to be censured, since it was not necessary and, therefore, not excusable.

Louis, then, made these five blunders: he extinguished the minor powers;[e] he increased the power of a ruler who was already powerful in Italy;[f] he brought into Italy a very strong foreign power;[g] he did not institute direct rule, and he did not set up colonies. Nevertheless, these mistakes need not have damaged him during his lifetime if he had not committed a sixth: that of putting down the Venetians.[h] For if he had neither aggrandised the Church nor brought the King of Spain into Italy, it would have been reasonable and necessary to put them down. But since he had followed these first two courses, he should never have

[a] In May 1502, Cesare Borgia moved to attack Florence, but was impeded by troops sent by Louis XII to help the Florentines.]

[b] In July 1501; but to attack the Spaniards in the Kingdom of Naples (see p. 27), not to check Cesare Borgia's growing power.]

[c] By the Treaty of Granada (11 Nov. 1500), Louis and Ferdinand the Catholic agreed to conquer the Kingdom of Naples; Campania and Abruzzi were to go to France, Apulia and Calabria to Spain.]

[d] I.e., the existing ruler, Frederick I of Aragon.]

[e] The Marquis of Mantua and the others mentioned on p. 12.]

[f] Alexander VI.]   [g] Ferdinand the Catholic.]

[h] France entered the League of Cambrai (Dec. 1508) against Venice, which was decisively defeated at Vailà (or Agnadello) on 14 May 1509.]

permitted the ruin of the Venetians. Since the Venetians were power-ful, they would always have prevented the other powers from in-tervening in Lombardy; they would never have permitted intervention if they were not to become masters of Lombardy themselves. And the other powers would not have wanted to take Lombardy from the King of France in order to give it to the Venetians, and they would not have had the strength to fight against both France and Venice. If anyone should urge that Louis ceded the Romagna to Alexander, and the Kingdom of Naples to the King of Spain, in order to avoid waging war, I should reply with the arguments advanced before: that one should never permit troubles to develop in order to avoid having to fight a war; because it is never in fact avoided but only postponed to your detri-ment. And if others should cite the promise the King made to the Pope (to undertake that campaign[a] for him in return for the annulling of his marriage and making Rouen[b] a cardinal), I would reply with arguments I shall advance later about how rulers should keep their promises.[c]

King Louis, then, lost Lombardy because he did not follow any of the policies followed by those who have annexed countries and been determined to keep them. And there is nothing extraordinary about this; it is a matter of course and to be expected.

I discussed this matter at Nantes[d] with the Cardinal of Rouen, when the Duke Valentino (as Cesare Borgia, the son of Pope Alexander, was commonly called) was engaged in capturing the Romagna. When the Cardinal of Rouen remarked to me that Italians did not understand warfare, I replied that the French did not understand statecraft, for if they did they would not have permitted the Church to acquire so much power. And experience has shown that the power of both the Church and of the King of Spain, here in Italy, has been brought about by the King of France, and they have brought about his ruin.[e]

From this may be derived a generalisation, which is almost always valid: anyone who enables another to become powerful, brings about his own ruin. For that power is increased by him either through guile or through force, and both of these are reasons for the man who has become powerful to be on his guard.

[a In the Romagna.]
[b His marriage to Jeanne de Valois; Georges d'Amboise, archbishop of Rouen.]
[c See pp. 61–3.]   [d In 1500.]
[e I.e., the collapse of French power in Italy.]

CHAPTER IV

Why the Kingdom of Darius, conquered by Alexander, did not rebel against his successors after Alexander's death

Given the difficulties encountered in holding a newly conquered territory, the following facts may cause surprise. Alexander the Great became master of Asia within a few years[a] and, not long afterwards, died.[b] It might have been expected that the whole region would then rebel; nevertheless, Alexander's successors[c] held it, and had to contend with no other difficulties than those arising from their own ambitious schemes.

I reply that all principalities known to history have been ruled in one of two ways: either by one ruler, who is helped to govern the kingdom by others, who are in reality his servants, acting as ministers through his grace and favour; or else by a ruler and barons who hold that rank by hereditary right, not through the favour of the ruler. Such barons have their own territories and subjects, who recognise them as lords and are naturally devoted to them. In states governed by a ruler and his servants, the ruler has more authority, because throughout the country there is no one else who is recognised as a lord; and if the subjects obey others, it is because these are his ministers or officials, not because there is any personal devotion to them.

Contemporary examples of these two types of government are the Turkish Sultan and the King of France. The whole Turkish Kingdom is governed by one ruler, the others[d] all being his servants; and his Kingdom is divided into sanjaks,[e] to which he sends various administrators, whom he changes and moves as he pleases. But the King of France is placed amidst a great number of hereditary lords, recognised in that state by their own subjects, who are devoted to them. They have their own hereditary privileges, which the King disallows only at his peril. If these two kinds of state are considered, then, it will be found

---

[a Between 334 and 327 B.C.]   [b In 323 B.C.]
[c The seven Greek generals, from whose internecine conflicts eleven new kingdoms eventually emerged.]
[d I.e., the others who governed or administered the Kingdom.]
[e This was the name of the administrative districts.]

that it is difficult to overcome a state of the Turkish type but, if it has been conquered, very easy to hold it. On the other hand, in some respects it is easier to conquer a state like France, but it is very difficult to hold it.

The reasons why it is hard to conquer the Turkish Kingdom are, first, there is no possibility that princes[a] of the Kingdom will seek aid from a foreigner; secondly, there is no hope that the men surrounding the ruler will rebel, thus facilitating the invasion, for the reasons already mentioned. Since they are all servants and owe their position to him, it is harder to corrupt them, and if one does succeed, little advantage is to be hoped for, because they will not be followed by the inhabitants, for the reasons mentioned.

It follows that anyone who attacks the Sultan of Turkey must expect to find the enemy united, and will be obliged to trust more in the strength of his own troops than in the disunity of his enemy. But if victory is achieved, and the defeat inflicted is so decisive that the enemy forces cannot regroup, there remains no other obstacle except the ruler's family. If they are wiped out, there is no other focus of resistance to be feared, since no one else enjoys any standing with the inhabitants. And just as the conqueror could expect no help from them before his victory, afterwards he will have no reason to fear them.

The opposite occurs in kingdoms ruled like France, because it is easy for you to make headway, through winning over some barons of the kingdom (because there are always those who are disaffected and those who want to change the regime). For the reasons already given, they can assist your campaign and help you gain victory. Afterwards, when you want to keep what you have acquired, countless difficulties will be encountered, both from those who have helped you and from those who have suffered because of your invasion. It is not enough to wipe out the ruling family, since there remain these nobles, who are very ready to lead new revolts. Since you can neither satisfy nor destroy them, you will lose that state whenever circumstances are unfavourable.

Now, if the character of the government of Darius is borne in mind, it will be found that it resembles the Turkish Kingdom. And therefore Alexander was forced to make a frontal assault and win a decisive victory; afterwards, since Darius was dead, Alexander was able to

[a *principi*: they may be called 'princes', but they were really servants of the ruler.]

maintain his power securely, for the reasons given above. And if his successors had remained united, they could easily have retained their power; for the only tumults arising in that Kingdom resulted from their own conduct. But it is impossible to hold without difficulty states organised like France.

This explains why there were so many rebellions against the Romans in Spain, Gaul and Greece, for there were many principalities in these countries. While the memory of these principalities endured, the Romans could never be certain of keeping possession of these territories; but when it faded, after their own rule had been long established, their hold over them was assured. However, when the Romans later fell to fighting among themselves,[a] each leader of a faction was able to dominate a region of these countries, according to how much authority he acquired within it. And because their old hereditary ruling families no longer existed, these provinces recognised only the authority of various Roman leaders.

Bearing all these things in mind, then, nobody should be surprised how easy it was for Alexander to maintain his position in Asia, and how difficult it was for others to hold conquered territories, as Pyrrhus and many others discovered. This contrast does not depend upon how much ability the conquerors displayed but upon the different characteristics of the conquered states.

CHAPTER V

How one should govern cities or principalities that, before being conquered, used to live under their own laws

When states that are annexed have been accustomed to living under their own laws and in freedom,[b] as has been said,[c] there are three ways of holding them: the first, to destroy their political institutions; the second, to go to live there yourself;[d] the third, to let them continue to

[a During the civil war between Caesar and Pompey.]
[b See p. 109.] [c See p. 5.] [d I.e., instituting direct rule.]

live under their own laws, exacting tribute and setting up an oligarchical government that will keep the state friendly towards you. Since the government has been set up by that ruler, it knows that it will be dependent upon his goodwill and power, and will be very concerned to maintain the status quo. If one wants to preserve a city that is accustomed to being independent and having free institutions, it is more easily held by using its citizens to govern it than in any other way.

The Spartans and the Romans provide good examples. The Spartans held Athens[a] and Thebes[b] by establishing oligarchies there; yet they eventually lost control over them. In order to hold Capua, Carthage and Numantia, the Romans destroyed them[c] and consequently never lost them. They tried to hold Greece in a similar manner to the Spartans, by granting it freedom and letting it live under its own laws. This was unsuccessful, so they were then forced to destroy many cities in that country, in order to maintain their hold over it. In fact, destroying cities is the only certain way of holding them. Anyone who becomes master of a city accustomed to a free way of life, and does not destroy it, may expect to be destroyed by it himself, because when it rebels, it will always be able to appeal to the spirit of freedom and its ancient institutions, which are never forgotten, despite the passage of time and any benefits bestowed by the new ruler. Whatever he does, whatever provisions he makes, if he does not foment internal divisions or scatter the inhabitants, they will never forget their lost liberties and their ancient institutions, and will immediately attempt to recover them whenever they have an opportunity, as Pisa did after enduring a century of subjection to the Florentines.[d]

However, when cities or countries are accustomed to living under a prince, and the ruling family is wiped out, the inhabitants are used to obeying but lack their older ruler; they are unable to agree on making one of themselves ruler, and they do not know how to embrace a free

[a Following their victory in the Peloponnesian War, the Spartans in 404 B.C. imposed on Athens the government of the so-called Thirty Tyrants, which was overthrown in 403 by Thrasybulus, who restored democratic rule.]
[b The oligarchy established there lasted only three years (382–379 B.C.); it was overthrown by Pelopidas and Epaminondas.]
[c Carthage was destroyed in 146 B.C., Numantia in 133 B.C.; the political organisation of Capua was destroyed in 211 B.C.]
[d Pisa was bought from Gabriele Maria Visconti in 1405, subdued in 1406, and lost in 1494, the 'opportunity' (*accidente*) being the turmoil into which Charles VIII's invasion had thrown Italian politics.]

way of life.[a] Consequently, they are slow to resort to arms, and a ruler can more easily win them over, and be sure that they will not harm him.

But in republics there is greater vitality,[b] more hatred, and a stronger desire for revenge; they do not forget, indeed cannot forget, their lost liberties. Therefore, the surest way is to destroy them or else go to live there.[c]

CHAPTER VI

New principalities acquired by one's own arms and ability

Nobody should be surprised if, in discussing completely new principalities, both as regards the ruler and the type of government,[d] I shall cite remarkable men as examples. For men almost always follow in the footsteps of others, imitation being a leading principle of human behaviour. Since it is not always possible to follow in the footsteps of others, or to equal the ability of those whom you imitate, a shrewd man will always follow the methods of remarkable men, and imitate those who have been outstanding, so that, even if he does not succeed in matching their ability, at least he will get within sniffing distance of it. He should act as skilful archers do, when their target seems too distant: knowing well the power of their bow, they aim at a much higher point, not to hit it with the arrow, but by aiming there to be able to strike their target.

I maintain, then, that in a completely new principality, where there is a new ruler, the difficulty he will have in maintaining it will depend on how much ability he possesses. And because for a private citizen to become ruler presupposes that he is either able or lucky, it might seem that one or other of these would, to some degree, mitigate many of the difficulties. Nevertheless, rulers maintain themselves better if they owe little to luck. It is also very helpful when the ruler is compelled to go and live in his principality, because he does not possess other states.

[a Cf. *Disc.* II, 2.]   [b See esp. *Disc.* II, 2.]   [c See above p. 17 n. *d*.]
[d New both as to dynasty and as to political organisation.]

19

However, to come to those who have become rulers through their own ability[a] and not through luck or favour,[b] I consider that the most outstanding were Moses, Cyrus, Romulus, Theseus and others of that stamp. And although one should not discuss Moses, because he was merely an executor of what had been ordained by God, yet he should be admired even if only for that favour which made him worthy to speak with God. But let us consider Cyrus and others who have acquired or founded kingdoms. They will all be found remarkable, and if their actions and methods are considered, they will not appear very different from those of Moses, who had such a great master.

If their deeds and careers are examined, it will be seen that they owed nothing to luck except the opportunity to shape the material into the form that seemed best to them. If they had lacked the opportunity, the strength of their spirit would have been sapped; if they had lacked ability, the opportunity would have been wasted.

It was necessary, then, for Moses to find the people of Israel in Egypt, enslaved and oppressed by the Egyptians, so that they would be disposed to follow him, in order to escape from their servitude. It was necessary that Romulus, who was exposed at birth in Alba, did not find there full scope for his abilities, so that he should have wanted to become King of Rome and, indeed, its founder. It was necessary that Cyrus should have found the Persians discontented under the rule of the Medes, and that the Medes should have been soft and weak because of the long peace.[c] And Theseus could not have fully revealed his abilities had he not found the Athenians dispersed. These opportunities, then, permitted these men to be successful, and their surpassing abilities enabled them to recognise and grasp these opportunities; the outcome was that their own countries were ennobled and flourished greatly.

Those who, like them, become rulers through their own abilities, experience difficulty in attaining power, but once that is achieved, they keep it easily. The difficulties encountered in attaining power arise partly from the new institutions and laws they are forced to introduce in order to establish their power and make it secure. And it should be realised that taking the initiative in introducing a new form of government is very difficult and dangerous, and unlikely to succeed. The

[a M. now comes to the theme of this chapter.]
[b This is the theme of Ch. VII.]
[c The peace that lasted from 600 to 560 B.C.]

reason is that all those who profit from the old order will be opposed to the innovator, whereas all those who might benefit from the new order are, at best, tepid supporters of him. This lukewarmness arises partly from fear of their adversaries, who have the laws on their side, partly from the sceptical temper of men, who do not really believe in new things unless they have been seen to work well. The result is that whenever those who are opposed to change have the chance to attack the innovator, they do it with much vigour, whereas his supporters act only half-heartedly; so that the innovator and his supporters find themselves in great danger.

In order to examine this matter thoroughly, we need to consider whether these innovators can act on their own or whether they depend upon others; that is, whether they need to persuade others if they are to succeed, or whether they are capable of establishing themselves by force. In the former case, they always fare badly and accomplish nothing. But if they do not depend upon others and have sufficient forces to take the initiative, they rarely find themselves in difficulties. Consequently, all armed prophets[a] succeed whereas unarmed ones fail. This happens because, apart from the factors already mentioned, the people are fickle; it is easy to persuade them about something, but difficult to keep them persuaded. Hence, when they no longer believe in you and your schemes, you must be able to force them to believe.[b]

If Moses, Cyrus, Theseus and Romulus had been unarmed, the new order which each of them established would not have been obeyed for very long. This is what happened in our own times to Fra' Girolamo Savonarola, who perished together with his new order as soon as the masses began to lose faith in him; and he lacked the means of keeping the support of those who had believed in him, as well as of making those who had never had any faith in him believe.[c]

Such innovators, then, have to confront many difficulties; all the dangers come after they have begun their enterprises, and need to be overcome through their own ability. But once they have succeeded, and begin to be greatly respected (after they have extinguished those envious of their success), they remain powerful, secure, honoured and successful.

[a *profeti*: although this word is suggested by the cases of Moses and Savonarola, it refers not only to theocratic rulers but, as Russo notes, to all new rulers.]
[b To act as if they believed; in short, to obey.]
[c I.e., forcing them to support him or, at least, not to oppose him.]

I should like to add a less important example than the eminent ones already discussed. But it certainly is worthy of mention in this context, so let it suffice for all the others like it: I refer to Hiero of Syracuse. From being a private citizen, he became ruler of Syracuse. He enjoyed a fine opportunity but, apart from that, his success owed nothing to luck. For when the Syracusans were in desperate straits,*ᵃ* they chose him as their general; afterwards he was deservedly made their ruler. And even in private life he showed so much ability that it was written of him 'quod nihil illi deerat ad regnandum praeter regnum'.*ᵇ* He disbandedᶜ the old army and raised a new one; he abandoned the old alliances and formed new ones; and as soon as he possessed his own troops and had reliable allies he could build any edifice he wantedᵈ upon this foundation. Thus, it was very difficult for him to attain power, but not to keep it.

CHAPTER VII

New principalities acquired through the power of others and their favour

Private citizens who become rulers only through favour or luck achieve that rank with little trouble, but experience great difficulty in retaining it. In arriving at that position there are no problems, because they fly there; all the difficulties arise afterwards. This is the situation if a state or territory is granted to someone either for money or by favour of the giver, as happened to many in Greece, in the cities of Ionia and the Hellespont, where Darius set up rulers so that they would hold them to increase his security and enhance his glory.ᵉ Other cases are those private citizens who became emperors, attaining the imperial throne by bribing the soldiers.ᶠ Such men are entirely dependent on the goodwill

---

[ᵃ In 270 B.C., when they were attacked by the Mamertines.]

[ᵇ Justinus, XXIII, 4: 'that the only thing he lacked to be a ruler was a kingdom'. What Justinus wrote was: 'ut nihil ei regium deesse, praeter regnum videretur'.]

[ᶜ See p. 50.]   [ᵈ I.e., construct his state.]

[ᵉ M. alludes to the division of the Persian Empire into satrapies in the sixth century B.C.; 'Greece' refers not to the Greek mainland but, as M. specifies, to the Greek cities of Asia and the Hellespont.]

[ᶠ E.g., Ch. XIX *passim*.]

and prosperity of those who gave them their positions, and these are two things that are exceedingly variable and uncertain. Such men lack the knowledge and capacity to maintain their power. They lack the knowledge because, unless he has great intelligence and ability, it is not to be expected that a man who has always lacked direct experience of public life should know how to rule. They lack the capacity because they do not have devoted and loyal forces at their disposal. Moreover, like all other natural things that are born and grow rapidly, states that grow quickly cannot sufficiently develop their roots, trunks and branches, and will be destroyed by the first chill winds of adversity. This happens unless those who have so quickly become rulers have the ability to profit by what luck or favour has placed in their laps, and know how to make provision very speedily to preserve their power, developing afterwards the foundations that others have laid before they become rulers.

To illustrate these two methods of becoming ruler, namely, through ability or through favour or luck, I want to cite two recent examples: Francesco Sforza and Cesare Borgia. Francesco, through using appropriate methods[a] and exploiting his great ability, from being a private citizen became Duke of Milan; and he maintained with very little trouble the position that he attained only with countless difficulties. On the other hand, Cesare Borgia, popularly called the Duke Valentino, attained his position through the favour and help of his father, and lost it when these disappeared,[b] despite having used every means and having done all those things that a far-seeing and able man should do, in order to put down his roots in territories that he had acquired thanks to the power and favour of others. For, as I have said, a man who does not lay his foundations at first may be able to do it later, if he possesses great ability, although this creates difficulties for the builder and the edifice itself may well prove unstable.[c]

If the whole career of the Duke is considered, then, it will be seen that he succeeded in laying very strong foundations for his future power. I do not consider it superfluous to discuss it, for I do not know what better precepts to offer to a new ruler than to cite his actions as a pattern; and although his efforts were in the end unsuccessful, he should not be blamed, because it resulted from extraordinarily bad luck.

[a] I.e., double-dealing or treachery: see *Arte d. guerra*, Bk I; *Ist. fior.* IV, 24 *et seq.*]
[b] I.e., when Alexander VI died, in 1503.]
[c] *edificio*: i.e., the state or government constructed.]

23

In seeking to make his son the Duke a great man, Alexander VI faced many difficulties, both present and future. First, he did not see how he could make him a ruler of any territory that was not part of the States of the Church. And if he were to appropriate one of the territories belonging to the Church, he was well aware that the Duke of Milan*a* and the Venetians would not permit it (for Faenza and Rimini were already under the protection of the Venetians). Apart from this problem, Alexander saw that the Italian military forces (and especially those that he could have used most easily) belonged to those who had every reason to fear any increase of the Pope's power; therefore, he could not safely use them, because they all belonged to the Orsini and Colonna factions and their adherents.*b*

It was therefore necessary to sow disorder in Italy, making their states unstable, so as to be able to seize and hold some portion of them. This was easy for him, because he found that the Venetians, for other reasons, wanted to bring the French back into Italy. Not only did he not oppose this policy; he facilitated it by annulling the first marriage of King Louis.*c* The King, then, invaded Italy with the help of the Venetians and the consent of Alexander. Louis was no sooner in Milan*d* than the Pope received troops from him for his own campaign in the Romagna, which was made easier because of the standing of the King.

After the Duke had conquered the Romagna*e* and defeated the Colonna faction, two things hindered him from holding that region securely and annexing more territory. One was that he had doubts about the loyalty of his troops, the other was the goodwill of the King of France. The Orsini troops, which he had used, might prove worthless when he attacked and not only prevent him from annexing more territory, but take from him what he had acquired. He also feared that the King might deprive him of what he possessed.

He had a proof of the worth of the Orsini troops when, after having besieged Faenza,*f* he attacked Bologna, because he saw them under-

---

[*a* Ludovico Sforza.]   [*b* See pp. 41–2.]   [*c* See p. 14 n. *b*.]   [*d* 6 Oct. 1499.]
[*e* This campaign lasted from Nov. 1499 until Jan. 1503.]
[*f* 25 April 1501.]

take that attack half-heartedly.[a] And he understood the King's attitude when, after he had captured the Duchy of Urbino,[b] he attacked Tuscany, for the King made him abandon the campaign.

The Duke then decided not to depend any longer upon the troops and the favour of others. He first undermined the strength of the Orsini and Colonna factions in Rome, by making all their noble adherents his own nobles, heaping much wealth on them. He also honoured them, according to their merits, giving them military posts and responsibilities. The outcome was that within a few months they abandoned their ancient factional loyalties, and became completely attached to the Duke.

After this, he waited for an opportunity to destroy the leaders of the Orsini faction, having already scattered those of the Colonna. A fine chance came, and he exploited it to the full. For the Orsini leaders realised, belatedly, that the great power of the Duke and of the Church spelt their ruin, and called a diet at Magione, in the province of Perugia.[c] This meeting gave rise to the revolt in Urbino[d] and disorders in the Romagna, and countless other dangers for the Duke,[e] all of which he overcame with the help of the French.

This restored his prestige, but he distrusted the King of France and all other external forces; in order not to risk depending on them, he resorted to trickery. He so cleverly concealed his intentions that the Orsini leaders, through the person of the Signor Paulo,[f] became reconciled with him. The Duke treated Paulo very courteously and generously, giving him money, fine clothes and horses, in order to reassure him. Their naivety was such that it brought them to Senigallia, and into the hands of the Duke.[g] Having killed these leaders, then, and

[a] A few days later; Borgia was then compelled to come to terms with Giovanni Bentivoglio.]

[b] 21 June 1502.]   [c] 9 Oct. 1502.]

[d] In fact, this began two days before, on 7 Oct., and within a few days Guido Ubaldo Montefeltro repossessed the Duchy.]

[e] Borgia's troops were defeated on 17 Oct.]

[f] Paulo Orsini who, on behalf of the other leaders, met Cesare Borgia at Imola on 25 Oct.]

[g] On 31 Dec. 1502, Borgia had Vitellozzo Vitelli and Oliverotto Euffreducci strangled at Senigallia; and on 18 Jan. 1503 he had Paulo Orsini and the Duke of Gravina Orsini strangled at the Castel della Pieve. See M.'s *Description of the Methods Used by Duke Valentino when Killing Vitellozzo Vitelli, Oliverotto da Fermo, the Signor Pagolo and the Duke of Gravina Orsini.*]

won over their adherents to himself, the Duke had established a very good basis for his power, because he controlled all the Romagna, together with the Duchy of Urbino and, especially, he thought that the Romagna was well disposed towards him, and that he had won over all the inhabitants, for they had begun to enjoy prosperity.

Since this policy of his should be known about, and imitated by others, I do not want to pass over it. After the Duke had conquered the Romagna, he found that it had been controlled by violent lords, who were more disposed to despoil their subjects than to rule them properly,[a] thus being a source of disorder rather than of order; consequently, that region was full of thefts, quarrels and outrages of every kind. He considered it necessary to introduce efficient government, because he wanted the region to be peaceful and its inhabitants obedient to his monarchical authority. He therefore sent there messer Remirro de Orco, a cruel and energetic man, giving him full powers.[b] Remirro quickly restored order and peace, and acquired a very formidable reputation. Later, the Duke considered that such great power was undesirable, because he was afraid it would incur hatred; and he set up a civil tribunal[c] under a distinguished president,[d] in the centre of the region, to which each city sent a lawyer. Because he recognised that the severe measures that had been taken had resulted in his becoming hated by some people, in order to dispel this ill-feeling and win everyone over to him, he wanted to show that if any cruel deeds had been committed they were attributable to the harshness of his governor, not to himself. And availing himself of an appropriate opportunity, one morning[e] the Duke had Remirro placed in two pieces[f] in the square at Cesena, with a block of wood[g] and a blood-stained sword at his side. This terrible spectacle left the people both satisfied and amazed.

But let me continue from where I left off. I say that the Duke was very powerful, and secure in some measure against existing dangers, because he possessed his own troops,[h] and had largely destroyed those neighbouring forces that could have harmed him. Since he wanted to

[a There is a longer account in *Disc.* III, 29.]
[b In 1501.]   [c In Oct. 1502.]
[d Antonio Ciocchi da Montesansavino, also known as Antonio dal Monte.]
[e 26 Dec. 1502; Remirro had been arrested on 22 Dec.]
[f Probably decapitated.]
[g *uno pezzo di legno*: lit., 'a piece of wood'; almost certainly an execution block.]
[h Cf. p. 49.]

annex more territory, he had to be very careful about the King of France. For he recognised that the King, who had belatedly realised his mistake,[a] would not tolerate this plan. The Duke therefore began to seek new alliances, and to temporise with the King of France when the French undertook a campaign in the Kingdom of Naples against the Spaniards, who were besieging Gaeta.[b] His aim was to protect himself against them;[c] if Alexander had not died, he would soon have succeeded.

This was how he acted in relation to the existing situation. But as to the future, his main fear was that a new pope might be hostile to him, and seek to take away what Alexander had given to him. He decided to protect himself against this possibility by following four courses of action: first, to wipe out the families of the rulers whom he had dispossessed, so that a new pope could not restore them to power; secondly, to win over all the Roman nobles, as has been said, so that by using them he could check a new pope;[d] thirdly, to have the college of cardinals as well disposed towards him as possible; fourthly, to extend his power so much, before the Pope died, that he would be capable of resisting the first attacks without outside aid. Of these four aims, he had achieved three by the time Alexander died, and had almost achieved the fourth. For he had killed as many of the old dispossessed rulers[e] as he was able, and very few escaped from him. He had won over the Roman nobles, and most of the cardinals. As for annexing new territories, he had planned to become master of Tuscany, he already held Perugia and Piombino,[f] and had taken Pisa under his protection. And since he no longer needed to be worried by French power (which was indeed now the case, as the French had already been deprived of the Kingdom of Naples by the Spaniards, with the result that each of them would have been obliged to purchase an alliance with him) he would swoop on Pisa. After this, Lucca and Siena would have surrendered immediately, partly through envious hatred of the Florentines, partly through fear; and the Florentines could have done nothing. If he had succeeded in all this (and it could well have happened within the very

[a I.e., of underrating Cesare Borgia.]
[b In 1503.]   [c I.e., the French.]   [d See pp. 40–1.]
[e *signori*; but, as specified earlier, M. meant their descendants, esp. the males. See pp. 129, 139.]
[f He conquered Perugia on 6 Jan. 1503, Piombino on 3 Sept. 1501.]

year that Alexander died), he would have acquired so much military strength and so much prestige that he would have been solidly established in power, and would no longer have depended on the favour and arms of others, but on his own strength and ability.

However, five years after the Duke had taken up the sword, Alexander died.[*a*] He found himself firmly established only in the Romagna, with all his other possessions in the air, between two very powerful enemy armies,[*b*] and critically ill. But the Duke possessed such indomitable spirit and so much ability, he was so well aware that men must either be won over or else destroyed, and had such a sound basis for his power, which he had established in such a short period, that he would have overcome all the difficulties if he had not had those armies on top of him, or if he had been in good health.

That his power was firmly based is shown by the following facts. The Romagna waited for him for more than a month.[*c*] In Rome no attack was made on him, even though he was half-dead; and although the Baglioni, Vitelli and Orsini came to Rome, they were unable to stir anyone up against him. Moreover, if he was not able to have whatever cardinal he wanted chosen pope, at least he was able to prevent someone he objected to from being chosen. Everything would have been easy for him, if he had been well when Alexander died. And he told me himself, on the day Julius II was elected,[*d*] that he had thought about what might happen when his father died, and had provided against everything, except that he had never thought that, when his father was dying, he too would be at death's door.

Having reviewed all the actions of the Duke, then, I would not wish to criticise him; rather, he seems to me worthy to be held up as a model, as I have done, for all those who have risen to power through favour or luck and through the arms of others. For he could not have acted differently, given that he possessed a great spirit and had high ambitions. Only two things hindered his schemes: the shortness of Alexander's pontificate[*e*] and his own illness.

Hence, anyone who considers it necessary in his new principality to

[*a* On 18 Aug. 1503.]   [*b* The Spaniards in Gaeta, the French in Rome.]
[*c* Several cities there submitted only when it was known that Borgia was held as a prisoner of Gonzalo Fernandez de Còrdoba.]
[*d* 28 Oct. 1503. The ailing Pius III had reigned briefly after Alexander's death (22 Sept.–18 Oct.), and M. had been sent to Rome in late October to follow the conclave.]
[*e* *vita*: lit., 'life'. Alexander was over seventy when he died. See also p. 41 n. *a*.]

deal effectively with his enemies, to gain allies, to conquer (whether by force or by cunning), to inspire both devotion and respectful fear in the people, to be obeyed and respectfully feared by troops, to neutralise or destroy those who can or must be expected to injure you, to replace old institutions with new ones, to be both severe and kind, both magnanimous and open-handed, to disband disloyal troops and form a new army, to maintain alliances with kings and other rulers in such a way that they will either be glad to benefit you or be slow to injure you: for all these, no better examples can be cited than the actions of this man.

He can be criticised only with regard to the election of Pope Julius, in which he made a bad choice; as has been said, even if he could not ensure that the man he favoured was made pope, he could have prevented certain other choices. And he should never have permitted any cardinals he had injured to be chosen, or any who, once he became pope, would have reason to be afraid of him. For men harm others because they fear them or because they hate them. Among those whom he had injured were San Piero ad Vincula, Colonna, San Giorgio and Ascanio;[a] if any of the others had become pope, they would have been afraid of him, with the exceptions of Rouen[b] and the Spaniards (the latter because of the bonds of relationship and obligation, the former because of his power, since he was supported by the Kingdom of France). The most important thing for the Duke, therefore, was to make a Spaniard pope and, if this was impossible, he should have arranged for Rouen to be chosen and not San Piero ad Vincula. Anyone who thinks that new benefits make important men forget old injuries is mistaken.[c] The Duke, then, blundered in this election, and it was the cause of his final downfall.

[a I.e., Giuliano della Rovere (Julius II), Giovanni Colonna, Raffaello Riario, Ascanio Sforza. The first and third of these are called by the names of their titular churches.]
[b Georges d'Amboise, archbishop of Rouen.]
[c Cf. *Disc.* III, 4.]

CHAPTER VIII

Those who become rulers through wicked means

But because there still remain two ways in which one can become a ruler, which cannot be attributed entirely either to favour or luck or to ability,[a] I do not want to neglect them, even though one of them could be discussed at greater length when dealing with republics.[b] These two ways are seizing power through utterly wicked means, and a private citizen becoming ruler of his country through the favour of his fellow-citizens. Considering the first way now,[c] I shall cite two examples, one ancient and the other modern, without considering explicitly the merits of this way of gaining power, for I think they should be enough for anyone who needs to imitate them.

Agathocles the Sicilian,[d] who became King of Syracuse, was not only an ordinary citizen,[e] but of the lowest and most abject origins. He was the son of a potter, and he always led a very dissolute life. Nevertheless, his evil deeds were combined with such energy of mind and body that, after having entered the militia, he rose through the ranks to become praetor[f] of Syracuse. Holding that position, he resolved to become ruler, and to hold violently and without being beholden to others the power that had been conferred on him. In order to achieve this purpose, he conspired with Hamilcar the Carthaginian, who was campaigning in Sicily. One morning he called together the people and the senate of Syracuse, as if some matter concerning the republic had to be decided. Then, at a prearranged signal, his soldiers killed all the senators and the richest men of the city. After this massacre, he seized control of the city, and thereafter held it without any civil strife.

Although he was twice defeated by the Carthaginians, and eventually besieged by them, he not only showed himself capable of defending his besieged city but, leaving part of his army to resist the siege, he attacked Africa with the rest. Very soon he was able to relieve Syracuse from the

[a M. refers to Chs. VI and VII.]   [b Cf. *Disc.* I, 52; III, 8, 34.]
[c The other is the theme of Ch. IX.]
[d M.'s account of Agathocles, which follows closely Bk XXII of Justinus's history, is not always accurate.]
[e *di privata fortuna*: i.e., he did not belong to a family prominent in public life.]
[f I.e., commander of the army.]

siege, and went on to reduce Carthage to the direst straits. Consequently, the Carthaginians were forced to make an agreement with him, according to which they were to remain in Africa and leave Sicily to Agathocles.[a]

If Agathocles's conduct and career[b] are reviewed, then, it will be seen that luck or favour played little or no part in his success, since (as has been said above) it was not through anyone's favour, but through overcoming countless difficulties and dangers, that he rose up through the ranks of the militia, and gained power, which he afterwards maintained by undertaking many courageous and dangerous courses of action.

Yet it cannot be called virtue[c] to kill one's fellow-citizens, to betray one's friends, to be treacherous, merciless and irreligious; power may be gained by acting in such ways, but not glory.[d] If one bears in mind the ability displayed by Agathocles in confronting and surviving dangers, and his indomitable spirit in enduring and overcoming adversity, there is no reason for judging him inferior to even the ablest general. Nevertheless, his appallingly cruel and inhumane conduct, and countless wicked deeds, preclude his being numbered among the finest men. One cannot, then, attribute either to luck or favour or to ability[e] what he achieved without either.

In our own times, when Alexander VI was pope, Oliverotto of Fermo,[f] whose father died when he was very young, was brought up by Giovanni Fogliani, his maternal uncle, and when still a youth was sent to train as a soldier under Paulo Vitelli, with a view to his achieving high rank when he had become proficient in things military. After Paulo's execution,[g] he trained under Vitellozzo, Paulo's brother; and since he was clever, and strong in body and spirit, in a very short time he became a leader of Vitellozzo's troops. But because he considered it demeaning

[a Not all of Sicily, but only the Greek part.]
[b *vita*: a reading proposed by Gerber, and accepted by Casella; Lisio: *virtù*.]
[c *virtù*: this word is used in several senses in M.'s account of Agathocles; usually it denotes 'energy', 'drive', 'ability' or 'courage', but here it has overtones, at least, of 'moral virtue'.]
[d Cf. *Disc.* III, 40.]
[e *virtù*: M. did not mean that Agathocles lacked *virtù* (in the senses of 'ability', 'energy' or 'courage'), but that it was through wicked means (*scelleratezze*) that he became ruler.]
[f Oliverotto Euffreducci. This is a rather loose sentence; it was his association with the Vitelli brothers and his seizure of Fermo that took place during Alexander's pontificate, not his early upbringing by his uncle.]
[g On 1 Oct. 1499. See p. 45.]

to serve under another, he resolved to seize power in Fermo, with Vitellozzo's assistance, and with the help of some citizens of Fermo, to whom the servitude of their native city was preferable to its free institutions.ᵃ Accordingly, he wrote to Giovanni Fogliani, saying that since he had been away from home for many years, he wanted to come to see him and his own city, and to inspect in some measure his own patrimony. Since achieving honour had been the only goal of all his efforts, so that his fellow-citizens would realise that he had not spent his time in vain, he wanted to return in a way that did him honour, and accompanied by a hundred cavalrymen drawn from his friends and followers. And he beseeched Giovanni to arrange for him to be received with due honour by the citizens of Fermo; this would not only honour himself, but also Giovanni, who had educated him.

Giovanni did not fail to treat his nephew with the utmost courtesy, and after the citizens (thanks to Giovanni) had received him with every honour, he was lodged in Giovanni's house, where, after he had spent some days secretly arranging everything that was necessary for carrying out his intended crime, Oliverotto held a formal banquet,ᵇ to which he invited Giovanni Fogliani and all the leading citizens of Fermo. After the banquet, and all the entertainments customary on such occasions, Oliverotto artfully raised some serious matters, speaking of the great power of Pope Alexander and his son Cesare, and of their various enterprises. When Giovanni and the others began to reply to what Oliverotto had said, he suddenly arose, saying that such matters should be discussed in a more private place. And he went into another room, followed by Giovanni and all the others. No sooner were they all seated than his soldiers emerged from hiding-places, and killed Giovanni and all the others.

After this massacre, Oliverotto mounted his horse and rode through the city, taking possession of it, and besieged the chief magistrates in their palace. They were so afraid that they felt constrained to obey him, and they formed a new government, of which he made himself the head. And when he had killed all the malcontents who could have

[ᵃ *la libertà*: Fermo was a free commune or republic. M. should not be understood to have meant that they really 'preferred' (*era più cara*) Fermo's servitude as such (i.e., its subjection to a princely ruler like Oliverotto); rather (as Sasso suggests) they were doubtless prominent citizens who hoped to have greater weight under a ruler whom they had helped to attain power.]
[ᵇ On 26 Dec. 1501, the second feast of Christmas, which provided a good pretext.]

harmed him, he consolidated his power by means of new civil and military institutions, so that in the space of the year that he held power he was not only secure in the city of Fermo, but made all the neighbouring powers fear him. And ousting him would have been as difficult as ousting Agathocles, if he had not let himself be tricked by Cesare Borgia, when the Orsini leaders and Vitellozzo Vitelli were captured (as was previously related)[a] at Senigallia. He too was captured there, a year after his parricide, and together with Vitellozzo, his former mentor in prowess and villainy, strangled.

It may well be wondered how it could happen that Agathocles, and others like him, after committing countless treacherous and cruel deeds, could live securely in their own countries for a long time, defend themselves against external enemies and never be plotted against by their citizens. For many others have not been able to maintain their power by acting cruelly even in peaceful times let alone in times of war, which are always uncertain.

I believe that this depends upon whether cruel deeds are committed well or badly. They may be called well committed (if one may use the word 'well' of that which is evil) when they are all committed at once, because they are necessary for establishing one's power, and are not afterwards persisted in, but changed for measures as beneficial as possible to one's subjects. Badly committed are those that at first are few in number, but increase with time rather than diminish. Those who follow the first method can in some measure remedy their standing both with God and with men, as Agathocles did. Those who follow the second cannot possibly maintain their power.

Hence, it should be noted that a conqueror, after seizing power, must decide about all the injuries he needs to commit, and do all of them at once, so as not to have to inflict punishments every day. Thus he will be able, by his restraint, to reassure men and win them over by benefiting them. Anyone who does not act in this way, either because he is timid or because he lacks judgement, will always be forced to stand with sword in hand. He will never be able to rely upon his subjects,[b] for they can never feel safe with him, because of the injuries that continue to be inflicted. For injuries should be done all together so that, because they are tasted less, they will cause less resentment;[c]

[a See p. 25.]   [b As M. advises rulers to do on p. 36.]
[c I.e., to those who are not 'injured', and who would otherwise be afraid or hostile.]

33

benefits should be given out one by one, so that they will be savoured more. And above all a ruler must live with his subjects in such a way that no unexpected events, whether favourable or unfavourable, will make him change course. For when difficult times put you under pressure you will not have enough time to take harsh measures, and any benefits that you confer will not help you, because they will be considered to be done unwillingly, and so you will receive no credit for them.

CHAPTER IX

The civil principality

I turn now to the other case,ᵃ when a private citizen becomes ruler of his own country through the favour of his fellow-citizens, not through villainy or intolerable violence of other kinds:ᵇ this may be called a civil principality (and to attain it, it is not necessary to have only ability or only good luck, but rather a lucky astuteness).ᶜ I say that one rises to this position either through being favoured by the people or through being favoured by the nobles;ᵈ for these two classes are found in every city.ᵉ And this situation arises because the people do not want to be dominated or oppressed by the nobles, and the nobles want to dominate and oppress the people. And from these two different dispositions there are three possible outcomes in cities: a principality, a republicᶠ or anarchy.

This kind of principality is brought about either by the people or by the nobles, according to whether one or the other has the opportunity

[ᵃ That mentioned at the beginning of Ch. VIII.]
[ᵇ The theme of Ch. VIII.]
[ᶜ *una astuzia fortunata*: being favoured by others is one kind of *fortuna* (see pp. 104–6) and such favour may be cleverly obtained. Russo suggests that M. may have had in mind the Medici. On the rise of this family to power, see *Disc.* I, 33, 52; *Ist. fior.* IV, 26; VII, 2, 10.]
[ᵈ *grandi*: i.e., those prominent in public life or politics; also called *i nobili, la nobiltà, uomini potenti*, etc. On the endemic conflict between the *populo* and the *grandi*, see *Disc.* I, 5; *Ist. fior.* III, 1.]
[ᵉ *città*: i.e., 'city' or 'city-state'.]
[ᶠ *libertà*: for M., a 'republic' is characterised by its 'liberty', i.e., free institutions or a free way of life, *uno vivere libero e civile*, as he often calls it in the *Discourses*.]

to act. As for the nobles, when they are unable to resist popular pressure, they begin to favour and advance one of themselves, and make him ruler so that, under his protection, they will be able to satisfy their appetites. On the other hand, the people, when they realise that they cannot resist the nobles, favour and advance one of themselves, and make him ruler, so that through his authority he will be able to protect them.

A man who becomes ruler through the help of the nobles will find it harder to maintain his power than one who becomes ruler through the help of the people, because he is surrounded by many men who consider that they are his equals, and therefore he cannot give them orders or deal with them as he would wish. On the other hand, a man who becomes ruler through popular support finds himself standing alone, having around him nobody or very few not disposed to obey him.

Moreover, the nobles cannot be satisfied if a ruler acts honourably, without injuring others. But the people can be thus satisfied, because their aims are more honourable than those of the nobles: for the latter want only to oppress and the former only to avoid being oppressed. Furthermore, a ruler can never protect himself from a hostile people, because there are too many of them; but he can protect himself from the nobles, because there are few of them. The worst that can befall a ruler from a hostile people is being deserted by them; but he has to fear not only being abandoned by hostile nobles, but also that they will move against him. Since they are more far-seeing and cunning, they are able to act in time to save themselves, and seek to ingratiate themselves with the one whom they expect to prevail. Again, a ruler is always obliged to co-exist with the same people, whereas he is not obliged to have the same nobles, since he is well able to make and unmake them at any time, advancing them or-reducing their power, as he wishes.

To clarify this matter, let me say that two main considerations need to be borne in mind with regard to the nobles. Either they conduct themselves in a way that links your success with theirs, or they do not. You should honour and esteem those of the former who are not rapacious. As for those who do not commit themselves to you, two different kinds of reason for their conduct must be distinguished. If they act in this way because of pusillanimity or natural lack of spirit, you should make use of them, especially those who are shrewd, because in good times they will bring you honour, and in troubled times you will have nothing to fear from them. But if they do not commit themselves to you calculatingly and because of ambition, it is a sign that they are thinking more of their own interests than of yours. And a ruler must watch these nobles very carefully, and fear them as much as if they were declared enemies, because if he finds himself in trouble they will always do their best to bring him down.

A man who becomes ruler through popular favour, then, must keep the people well disposed towards him. This will be easy, since they want only not to be oppressed. But a man who becomes ruler against the wishes of the people, and through the favour of the nobles, must above all else try to win over the people, which will be easy if you protect them. And if men are well treated by those from whom they expected ill-treatment, they become more attached to their benefactor; the people will at once become better disposed towards him than if he had attained power through their favour. A ruler can win over the people in many ways; but because these vary so much according to the circumstances one cannot give any definite rules, and I shall therefore leave this matter on one side. I shall affirm only that it is necessary for a ruler to have the people well disposed towards him; otherwise, in difficult times he will find himself in desperate straits.

Nabis, ruler of the Spartans, withstood a siege by all the other Greek powers and by a triumphant Roman army, defending both his country and his own power against them.[a] When danger threatened, he needed only to act against a few;[b] but if the people had been hostile to him, this would not have been enough. And doubt should not be cast on my opinion by quoting the trite proverb, 'He who builds upon the people, builds upon mud.' This is true if it is a private citizen who builds his power upon them, and believes that the people will come to his rescue if he is oppressed by his enemies or by the rulers. In such circumstances one may often be disappointed, as the Gracchi were in Rome and messer Giorgio Scali in Florence. But if it is a ruler who builds his power upon the people, and if he knows how to command and if he is courageous, does not despair in difficult times, and maintains the morale of his people by his spiritedness and the measures that he takes,

[a Against the Achaean League, as an ally of Philip V of Macedon. Cf. Livy, XXXIV, 22–40.]

[b Few 'of his subjects' is implied. Nabis favoured the people at the expense of the nobles, and Livy (XXXIV, 27) relates that he imprisoned and then killed about eighty prominent young men.]

he will never find himself let down by them, and he will realise he had laid sound foundations for his power.

These civil principalities tend to encounter grave difficulties if an attempt is made to transform them into absolute regimes.[a] For civil rulers either rule directly or through public officials. In the latter case their position is weaker and more dangerous, because they depend completely on the goodwill of those citizens who act as their officials. And, especially in troubled times, they can very easily remove him from power, either by moving against him or simply by refusing to obey him. Moreover, in troubled times, the ruler does not have enough time to assume absolute authority, because the citizens or subjects, accustomed as they are to obeying the officials, will not be disposed to obey him in such a crisis. And in difficult times, he will always lack men on whom he can depend.

For such a ruler cannot rely upon what he sees happen in peaceful times, when citizens have need of his government, because then everyone comes running, everyone is ready with promises, and everyone wants to die for him, when the prospect of death is far off.[b] But in troubled times, when the government needs the services of the citizens, few are then to be found. And it is especially dangerous to have to test their loyalty, because it can be done only once. A shrewd ruler, therefore, must try to ensure that his citizens, whatever the situation may be, will always be dependent on the government and on him; and then they will always be loyal to him.

CHAPTER X

How the strength of all principalities should be measured

There is another consideration that must be borne in mind when examining the strength of principalities: namely, whether a ruler has

---

[a These difficulties, then, are not inherent in 'civil principalities'; they arise if such a state is being changed into an 'absolute' regime, that is, a 'tyranny' (see *Disc.* I, 25).]
[b Cf. p. 59.]

sufficient territory and power to defend himself, when this is necessary, or whether he will always need some help from others.[a]

To clarify this matter, let me say that I consider that a ruler is capable of defending his state if he can put together an army that is good enough to fight a battle against any power that attacks it (either because he has many soldiers of his own or because he has sufficient money).[b] But a ruler who cannot confront any enemy on the field of battle, and is obliged to take refuge within the walls of his city, and keep guard over them, will always need to be helped by others.

The first case has already been discussed;[c] and later I shall say more about it.[d] No advice can be given with regard to the second case, except to exhort such a ruler to fortify and provision his city, and not seek to defend his rural territories. Others will be very slow to attack any ruler who fortifies his city well and deals with his subjects in the ways already discussed,[e] and to be considered later.[f] For men are always unwilling to undertake campaigns that they expect to be difficult; and it will never seem easy to attack a ruler who has his city well defended, and is not hated by the people.

The cities of Germany are completely independent, have little rural territory, and obey the Emperor only when they want to. They do not fear him or any other neighbouring power. The reason is that they are so well fortified that everyone considers that besieging them is necessarily a tiresome and difficult undertaking. For they all possess strong walls and adequate moats, and sufficient artillery; and they always ensure that their public storehouses contain enough food, drink and fuel to last for a year. Moreover, in order to maintain the common people without public expense, they always have enough raw materials to keep the people engaged for a year in those occupations essential to the life of the city, and which sustain the common people. They also consider military exercises to be very important, and have many regulations for maintaining them.

Therefore, a ruler who possesses a strong city and does not make

[a] This distinction has already been drawn in connection with 'innovators', or those seeking power (see p. 21).]
[b] To buy the services of mercenaries.]
[c] In Ch. VI.]   [d] In Chs. XII–XIV.]
[e] In Chs. VII and VIII, and esp. in IX, in which rulers are advised to keep the people well disposed towards them.]
[f] In Chs. XV–XIX and elsewhere.]

himself hated is safe from attack; and anyone who should attack him is eventually forced to beat an ignominious retreat. For so many unexpected things can happen in this world that it is virtually impossible to keep an army encamped idly in a siege for a whole year. It may be urged that if the people have properties outside the city, and see them destroyed, they will lose patience, and that the length of the siege and self-interested considerations[a] will sap their loyalty to their ruler. I reply that a strong and spirited ruler will always overcome such problems, by encouraging his subjects to believe that these evils will not last long, by warning them of the enemy's cruelty, and by dealing adroitly with those men who seem to him too outspoken.

Furthermore, it is to be expected that the enemy forces will burn and pillage the countryside when they arrive, and at a time when the spirits of the defenders are still high and they are determined to hold out. Therefore, after some days, the ruler has much less reason to be afraid, when the ardour of the defenders has cooled, the damage already done, the injuries already sustained, and there is nothing to be done. They are then much more likely to support their ruler, because they will consider that he is indebted to them, since it is in his defence that their homes have been burned and their properties ruined. And men are so constituted that they are as much bound by the benefits they confer as by those they receive. Hence, if the whole matter is carefully considered, it is clear that it should not be difficult for a shrewd ruler to keep up the morale of his citizens throughout any siege, provided that they do not lack the means necessary for sustaining life and defending themselves.

CHAPTER XI

Ecclesiastical principalities

It remains now[b] only to discuss ecclesiastical principalities, in which all the difficulties occur before they are acquired, for they are gained

---

[a] *la carità propria*: lit., 'self-love', conducing to love of one's possessions.]
[b] I.e., to complete the classification of the types of states, and ways of acquiring them, listed in Ch. I.]

either through ability or through favour or luck, and maintained without the help of either. This in turn is because they are sustained by ancient religious institutions, which have been sufficiently strong to maintain their rulers in office however they live or act. Only they have states and do not defend them, and subjects whom they do not trouble to govern; and although their states are undefended, they are not deprived of them. And their subjects, although not properly governed, do not worry about it; they cannot get rid of these rulers, nor even think about doing so. Only these principalities, then, are secure and successful.

However, since they are controlled by a higher power, which the human mind cannot comprehend, I shall refrain from discussing them; since they are raised up and maintained by God, only a presumptuous and rash man would examine them. Nevertheless, someone might ask me how it has happened that the temporal power of the Church has become so great, although before Alexander's[a] pontificate the leading Italian powers[b] (and not only those called 'powers', but every baron and lord, however unimportant) held this temporal power in little account, whereas now a King of France stands in awe of it, for it has been able to drive him out of Italy, and to ruin the Venetians. Accordingly it does not seem out of place to recall it, although it is well known.

Before King Charles of France invaded Italy,[c] this country was dominated by the popes, the Venetians, the King of Naples, the Duke of Milan and the Florentines. Each of these powers had two main preoccupations: first, that a foreign power should not invade Italy; secondly, that none of the other Italian powers should acquire more territory and power. Those who caused most concern were the popes and the Venetians. To limit the power of Venice, the others had to form an alliance, as happened in the defence of Ferrara.[d] And the Roman barons were used to limit papal power. As these were divided into two factions, the Orsini and the Colonna, they were always quarrelling among themselves, but carrying their arms under the very eyes of the popes, they kept the Papacy weak and ineffectual. And although there sometimes arose a spirited pope, such as Sixtus,[e] yet he could not

[a Alexander VI.]   [b I.e., Milan, Venice, Florence and Naples.]
[c Charles VIII; in 1494.]
[d In 1482 war broke out between Venice and Ercole I of Ferrara, who was supported by Milan and Florence. At the Peace of Bagnolo (1484), the autonomy of Ferrara was recognised, though the Polesine was ceded to Venice.]
[e Sixtus IV.]

overcome this problem, either because of the particular circumstances or because of lack of skill. The shortness of pontificates[a] was the reason, for it was very difficult to destroy one of the factions during the period of ten years that most popes reigned.[b] And if it happened that one pope almost succeeded in destroying the Colonna faction, the next pope would be hostile to the Orsini, which had the effect of reviving the Colonna faction, and yet he did not have enough time to destroy the Orsini faction. The result was that the temporal power of the Papacy was held in little regard in Italy.

Then Alexander VI came to the papal throne; more than any previous pope, he showed how much a pope could achieve through money and military means. Using the Duke Valentino,[c] and exploiting the opportunities provided by the French invasion, he did all those things which I have discussed above,[d] when considering the career of the Duke. And although Alexander's aim was to aggrandise the Duke, not the Church, nevertheless the outcome was to increase the power of the Church which, after his death, and the downfall of the Duke, became the beneficiary of his labours. Then came Pope Julius,[e] who found the Church already powerful, possessing all the Romagna, the Roman barons reduced to impotence, and their factions destroyed by the strong measures of Alexander. Moreover, Julius had opportunities for accumulating money never used before Alexander's time.[f] Julius not only followed these policies, he intensified them. He planned to capture Bologna,[g] to destroy the power of Venice, and to expel the French from Italy. All these enterprises were successful, and it was very much to his credit that he did everything in order to increase the power of the Church, and not any individual.[h] He kept the Orsini and Colonna factions in the same impotent condition in which he found them; and although they had some leaders capable of causing trouble, two factors militated against it. The first was the great power of

---

[a] *vita*: lit., 'life'. Cf. p. 87.]

[b] Of the immediately preceding popes, Sixtus IV reigned for thirteen years, Innocent VIII for eight, Alexander VI for eleven and Julius II for ten; only Pius III had a short pontificate (twenty-six days, in 1503).]

[c] Cesare Borgia.]   [d] In Ch. VII.]

[e] Julius II. M. disregards the very brief pontificate of Pius III, being concerned with the main tendencies of papal conduct.]

[f] Most commentators remark Julius's simoniacal proclivities; indeed Alexander had been notorious for these practices.]

[g] See *Disc.* I, 27.]   [h] Unlike Alexander (and other recent popes).]

41

the Church, which overawed them; the second was that there were no cardinals to lead either faction, the cause of the rivalries between them. These factions will always cause trouble whenever they have cardinals as leaders, because it is they who foster these factions, inside Rome and outside, and those barons are compelled to support their own factions. Thus, the ambition of prelates is at the root of the quarrels and tumults among the barons.

His Holiness Pope Leo,[a] then, has found the Papacy very powerful; and it is to be hoped that, just as his predecessors made it great by the use of force, he will make it very great and respected through his natural goodness and countless other virtues.

CHAPTER XII

The different types of army, and mercenary troops

I have discussed in detail all the different types of principality that I mentioned at the beginning,[b] and have given some consideration to the reasons for their prosperity and decline; and I have examined the ways in which many men have sought to acquire them and to hold them. I now turn to consider in a general way the means that can be used in attacking and defending them. I said earlier[c] how necessary it is for a ruler to have firm foundations for his power; otherwise, he will always come to grief. The main foundations of all states (whether they are new, old or mixed) are good laws[d] and good armies. Since it is impossible to have good laws if good arms are lacking,[e] and if there are good

---

[a Leo X.]   [b On. p. 5.]   [c E.g., pp. 23, 36–7.]

[d *le buone legge*: 'laws' here should probably not be understood in a narrow sense: rather M. had in mind 'laws' and 'customs' (or unwritten laws); in short, the factors making for political and social cohesion and stability.]

[e If the principality is not well defended, internal order cannot be maintained.]

arms there must also be good laws,[a] I shall leave laws aside and concentrate on arms.

I say, then, that the arms with which a ruler defends his state are his own, or they are mercenaries, or auxiliaries, or a mixture of all three. Mercenaries and auxiliaries are useless and dangerous; and anyone who relies upon mercenaries to defend his territories will never have a stable or secure rule. For they are disunited, ambitious,[b] undisciplined and treacherous; they are powerful when among those who are not hostile, but weak and cowardly when confronted by determined enemies; they have no fear of God, and do not maintain commitments with men. One's ruin is only postponed until the time comes when they are required to fight. In peaceful times you will be despoiled by them, in war by your enemies. The reason for all this is that they have no affection for you or any other reason to induce them to fight for you, except a trifling wage, which is not sufficient to make them want to risk their lives for you. They are very glad to be in your service as long as you do not wage war, but in time of war they either flee or desert. I should not need to spend very much time in arguing this case, since the present ruin of Italy has been caused by nothing else than the reliance over so many years on mercenary armies. Some of these mercenary armies were not ineffective, and they appeared powerful when fighting other mercenary armies, but when the foreign invasions began,[c] their real character was soon revealed. Thus, King Charles of France was permitted to conquer Italy with a piece of chalk;[d] and he who said that our sins were responsible[e] spoke the truth. However, they were not the sins that he meant, but those that I have specified; and because they were the sins of rulers, they too have been punished for them.[f]

---

[a] If 'laws' is understood in the usual sense, this would be false (for a country may possess a fine army and yet have laws that are censurable or a defective legal system). But if *buone legge* is understood in the sense of 'good order', M.'s position seems stronger. Cf. *Disc.* I, 4, in which M. says that 'when there is a good militia there must be good order' (*buono ordine*).]

[b] I.e., their leaders are 'ambitious'.]   [c] After 1494.]

[d] Commynes (*Mémoires*, VII, 14) attributes this witticism to Pope Alexander VI: they met with so little resistance that they had only to mark houses where their soldiers were to be billeted.]

[e] Savonarola, in a sermon preached before Charles VIII on 1 Nov. 1494, spoke of such sins as fornication, usury and cruelty as being responsible for the present 'tribulations'.]

[f] E.g., Ludovico Sforza, Piero de' Medici, Frederick I of Aragon, who relied on mercenaries.]

I want to show more effectively the defects of these troops. Mercenary generals are either very capable men, or they are not. If they are, you cannot trust them, because they will always be aspiring to achieve a great position for themselves, either by attacking you, their employer, or by attacking others contrary to your wishes. If they are mediocre, you will be ruined as a matter of course.

And if it is objected that anyone who has forces at his disposal (whether mercenaries or not) will act in this way,[a] I would reply by first drawing a distinction: arms are used either by a ruler or by a republic. If the former, the ruler should personally lead his armies, acting as the general. If the latter, the republic must send its own citizens as generals; and if someone is sent who turns out not to be very capable, he must be replaced; and if the general sent is capable, there should be legal controls that ensure that he does not exceed his authority. Experience has shown that only rulers and republics that possess their own armies are very successful, whereas mercenary armies never achieve anything, and cause only harm. And it is more difficult for a citizen to seize power in a republic that possesses its own troops than in one that relies upon foreign troops.

For many centuries both Rome and Sparta were armed and independent.[b] Today the Swiss are very well armed and completely independent. An example of the worth of ancient mercenaries is provided by the Carthaginians: they were attacked by their own mercenary troops after the first war against the Romans,[c] despite the fact that the generals were Carthaginians. Similarly, after the death of Epaminondas, the Thebans made Philip of Macedon general of their armies; and after he was victorious, he deprived them of their independence.[d] After the death of Duke Filippo,[e] the Milanese engaged Francesco Sforza to lead their armies against the Venetians. But when Sforza had defeated the Venetians at Caravaggio,[f] he joined forces with them and attacked

---

[a] I.e., as the 'very capable' generals do.]

[b] *libere*: it signifies primarily that they maintained their 'independence'; republican Rome also maintained its 'free institutions' (its *vivere libero*) but this cannot be said of Sparta.]

[c] In 346 B.C. Cf. *Disc.* III. 32.]

[d] *libertà*: see above, n. *b*. Philip conquered Thebes in 338 B.C., imposing an oligarchical government. However, he was not a mercenary; he had been an ally of the Thebans, leading the armies of the Thessalian and Theban League as early as 355.]

[e] Filippo Maria Visconti, on 13 Aug. 1447.]   [f] 15 Sept. 1448.]

the Milanese, who had been his employers. Sforza's own father,[a] who was employed as a general by Queen Giovanna of Naples, suddenly left her unprotected;[b] and, in order not to lose her Kingdom, she was forced to seek help from the King of Aragon.[c]

And although the Venetians and the Florentines augmented their dominions in the past by using mercenaries, and their generals did not seize power but defended them, my opinion is that in this matter the Florentines were very lucky; for some of the able generals who could have become a threat to them did not win victories, some met with opposition, and others went elsewhere to achieve their ambitions.

The general who did not conquer was John Hawkwood; his loyalty could not be put to the test, just because he did not win victories;[d] but everyone will acknowledge that if he had been victorious, the Florentines would have been at his mercy. The Sforza always had the Bracceschi troops[e] to contend with, and each faction checked the other: Francesco went to Lombardy to satisfy his ambitions, and Braccio moved against the Church and the Kingdom of Naples.

But let us turn to more recent events. The Florentines made Paulo Vitelli their general;[f] he was a very able man, who from modest beginnings had acquired a very high reputation. Nobody can deny that if he had captured Pisa, the Florentines would have been forced to retain his services because, if he had then become general of one of the armies of their enemies, the Florentines would have found themselves in desperate straits; and if they had retained him, he would have been in a commanding position.

If the conquests of the Venetians are reviewed, it is evident that they were secure and glorious when they fought their own wars (which was before they undertook campaigns in Italy), in which their nobles and the people in arms fought very skilfully and courageously. But when they began to fight on the mainland,[g] they forsook this very effective policy, and followed the Italian custom.[h] When they first began to expand their land empire, they had little reason to be afraid of their

---

[a Muzio Attendolo Sforza.]   [b c. 1421.]
[c Alfonso V ('the Magnanimous').]
[d The campaigns undertaken by Hawkwood were defensive in character.]
[e Those belonging to Andrea Fortebraccio.]   [f In June 1498.]
[g At the beginning of the fifteenth century, although Treviso had been annexed in 1339.]
[h I.e., of using mercenaries.]

mercenary generals, because not very much territory had yet been annexed and because the reputation of Venice was very high. But as they expanded further, under Carmagnola,*a* their blunder became evident. They knew that he was very able (since they had defeated the Duke of Milan under his command) but, on the other hand, they realised that he was pursuing the war*b* half-heartedly. They decided that they would not be able to win again by using his services (because he did not want to win), and yet they could not dismiss him without losing the territory that had been annexed. Hence, to protect themselves, they were forced to kill him.*c* Afterwards they had as generals Bartolomeo da Bergamo,*d* Roberto da San Severino,*e* the Count of Pitigliano*f* and others. With regard to these generals, what they had to fear was losing, not the dangers arising from their being victorious, as indeed happened later at Vailà*g* where, in a single battle,*h* they lost what they had gained with so much effort over eight hundred years.*i* For using mercenaries results only in slow, tardy and unimportant gains, but sudden and astonishing losses.

Since these examples have brought me to Italy,*j* which for many years has been controlled by mercenary armies, I want to examine them at greater length so that, when their rise and development have been surveyed, it will be easier to find a solution.

You must realise, then, how in recent times*k* the Empire began to lose much ground in Italy, the temporal power of the Papacy was greatly increased, and Italy came to be divided into many states. For in many of the large cities there were revolts against the nobles who (previously supported by the Emperor) had ruled oppressively, and the Church encouraged these revolts in order to increase its temporal power; and in

[*a* From 1426 onwards.]   [*b* Against Milan.]
[*c* He was tried, and executed on 5 May 1432.]
[*d* Bartolomeo Colleoni, who succeeded Carmagnola as general, and was defeated at Caravaggio (1448) by the Milanese, under Francesco Sforza.]
[*e* The Venetian general in the war against Ferrara (1482–84). See p. 6.]
[*f* Niccolò Orsini, the commander at Vailà.]
[*g* 4 May 1509: the battle of Vailà (or Vailate) or Agnadello, near Milan. Cf. *Disc.* I, 6; III, 31; *Ist. fior.* I, 29.]
[*h* *giornata*: it means 'battle', but it also lasted only one 'day'.]
[*i* It was a decisive defeat for the Venetians, though M. somewhat exaggerates the consequences.]
[*j* M. began by considering mercenaries in the Ancient World.]
[*k* Esp. during the fifteenth century.]

many other cities rulers had emerged from the ranks of the citizens. Hence, because Italy had largely come under the control of the Church and of some republics, and because these priests[a] and citizen-rulers had little experience of military matters, they all began to use outsiders to fight their battles.

Alberigo da Cunio,[b] a Romagnol, was the first to make these mercenary troops important. From this source other mercenary forces came to the fore, including those of Braccio and Sforza,[c] who in their day were the arbiters of Italy. After them came all the others who controlled mercenary armies up to our own times. And the result of their prowess has been that Italy has been overrun by Charles, plundered by Louis, ravaged by Ferdinand[d] and treated with contempt by the Swiss.[e] What happened, first, was that to enhance their own reputations, they neglected the infantry.[f] They did this because, since they were men who did not possess states of their own and lived by being mercenaries, small numbers of foot-soldiers did not enhance their position, and they were incapable of maintaining large numbers of them. Therefore, they resorted to having enough cavalry to maintain themselves and achieve a position of some importance. And things came to such a pass that an army of twenty thousand soldiers would contain scarcely two thousand foot-soldiers. Moreover, they employed all possible means to lessen the hardships and dangers, both to themselves and their troops, by inflicting few casualties in battle; instead, they took prisoners and did not demand ransoms. They did not attack fortified cities at night; mercenaries who defended cities were very reluctant to attack the besiegers; they did not fortify their camps with stockades or ditches; and they did not undertake sieges during winter. All these practices were permitted by the prevailing military code, and were adopted, as I have said, to avoid hardship and danger. The outcome of their activities is that Italy has become enslaved and despised.

---

[a] I.e., the popes.]

[b] Alberico da Barbiano, Count of Cunio, who died in 1409.]

[c] Andrea Fortebraccio and Muzio Attendolo Sforza.]

[d] Respectively, Charles VIII, Louis XII and Ferdinand the Catholic.]

[e] M. alludes esp. to the Swiss superiority at Novara (1500) and Ravenna (1512).]

[f] For M., the infantry should form the core of all armies: see *Arte d. guerra*, Bk I. These themes are discussed in more detail in *Disc.* II, 18.]

CHAPTER XIII

Auxiliaries, mixed troops
and native troops

Auxiliaries, which are the other kind of troops that are useless,^a are troops that are sent to you to aid and defend you, when you call on a powerful ruler for help. They were used recently by Pope Julius who, when he had seen the bad showing of his own mercenary troops in the campaign of Ferrara,^b resorted to auxiliaries, arranging with King Ferdinand of Spain that that ruler would help him with his own troops. In themselves, these auxiliaries can be capable and effective but they are almost always harmful to those who use them; for if they lose you will be ruined, and if they win you will be at their mercy.

Although ancient history provides many examples, I do want to discuss this recent case of Pope Julius II. His decision can only be judged rash: to put himself completely into the hands of a foreign ruler,^c in order to gain possession of Ferrara! But his good luck meant that he did not reap the fruits of his bad policy, for when the auxiliaries he was using were defeated at Ravenna,^d and the Swiss arrived^e and chased out the victors^f (contrary to what he and others had any reason to expect), he did not find himself at the mercy either of his enemies (who had fled) or of these auxiliaries, because the victory had been achieved by others,^g not by them. Again, the Florentines, because they were completely unarmed, brought ten thousand French troops to besiege Pisa:^h and this policy involved them in more danger than at any other time in their troubled history. Similarly, the Emperor of Constantinopleⁱ brought ten thousand Turkish troops in order to fight his fellow-Greeks;^j but when that war was finished^k they did not want to go

---

[^a As well as mercenaries.]   [^b In 1510. See p. 6.]
[^c I.e., Ferdinand the Catholic.]   [^d 11 April 1512.]
[^e At the end of May 1512.]   [^f The French.]
[^g By the Swiss.]   [^h In 1500.]
[ⁱ John Cantacuzene, Byzantine emperor.]
[^j During the civil war, which broke out in 1341 between the followers of John Cantacuzene and those of John Palaelogus.]
[^k In 1347.]

away, which marked the beginning of the servitude of Greece to the infidels.[a]

Therefore, anyone who wants to be unable to conquer should use such troops, because they are much more dangerous than mercenaries: for with them ruin is complete. They form a united force, and are used to obeying others.[b] But when mercenaries conquer, more time and greater opportunities are required before they will be in a position to do you harm. They do not form a united body, since they have been engaged and paid by you. And an outsider whom you appoint as their leader cannot at once assume such authority over them that harm to you will result. In short, with mercenaries, their cowardice or reluctance to fight[c] is more dangerous; with auxiliaries their skill and courage.

Wise rulers, then, always avoid using these troops, and form armies composed of their own men; and they prefer to lose using their own troops rather than to conquer through using foreign troops, for they do not consider a victory that is gained by using foreign forces to be genuine.

I never hesitate to cite Cesare Borgia and his actions. This Duke invaded the Romagna using auxiliaries (all his troops being French), and with them he captured Imola and Forlì.[d] But since he distrusted them, he then used mercenaries, which he thought less dangerous, employing the Orsini and Vitelli troops. When he later found them to be of doubtful value and loyalty, and therefore dangerous, he disbanded them[e] and formed an army composed of his own men.[f] And the difference between these kinds of army is very obvious if one compares the reputation of the Duke when he used only French troops or when he used the Orsini and Vitelli troops, and when he possessed his own soldiers, and was self-sufficient militarily. Then it became much greater, and he was never more esteemed than when everyone saw that he was the complete master of his own forces.

I am reluctant to cite examples that are neither Italian nor recent; nevertheless I must discuss Hiero of Syracuse, since I have already

---

[a Completed in 1453, when Constantinople fell.]

[b The ruler who sends them.]

[c *ignavia*: here it means both 'cowardice' and 'indolence' (reluctance to fight does not result only from cowardice).]

[d Between Nov. 1499 and Jan. 1500.]

[e Killing their leaders, and winning over the rest (see pp. 24–6).]

[f From the Romagna; but probably esp. the Orsini and Vitelli troops (see pp. 24–6).]

mentioned him.[a] As I said, after the Syracusans had made him leader of their army, he realised at once that those mercenary troops were useless, for they were condottieri of the same stamp as our Italian ones. And since he considered that he could not continue to employ them or disband them, he had them all cut to pieces.[b] Thereafter, he made war with his own troops and not foreign ones.

I want also to recall a relevant example from the Old Testament.[c] When David offered to Saul to go and fight Goliath, the Philistine champion, Saul gave him his own weapons and armour in order to imbue him with courage. But after David had put them on he rejected them, saying that he could not fight well with them, and he therefore wanted to confront the enemy with his own sling and knife. In short, weapons and armour belonging to others fall off you or weigh you down or constrict your movements.

After Charles VII (father of King Louis XI) had liberated France from the English,[d] through a combination of good luck and prowess, he recognised the need for France to be defended by national troops, and formed in his kingdom an army composed of cavalry and infantry.[e] His son Louis later disbanded the infantry,[f] and began to employ Swiss soldiers. This blunder being followed by the others,[g] led (as is indeed now obvious) to the present dangerous position of that Kingdom.[h] By strengthening the position of the Swiss, he demoralised the rest of his army, for he disbanded the infantry and made his own cavalry dependent on foreign soldiers. Since they are used to fighting together with the Swiss, they are not confident of being able to win battles without them. The outcome is that the French are inferior to the Swiss, and without the Swiss they make a poor showing against enemies. The French armies, then, have been of a mixed character, partly mercenary and partly national. Such a combination is much better than an army of auxiliaries or an army of mercenaries but much inferior to native troops. And let this example suffice: for the Kingdom of France would be unconquerable if the military system set up by Charles had been developed or, at least, preserved. But men have so little judgement and

---

[a See p. 22.]   [b Probably M. meant that Hiero killed only the mercenary leaders.]
[c I *Kings* xvii, 38–40.]   [d In 1453, at the end of the Hundred Years War.]
[e In fact, this was done earlier, between 1445 and 1448.]   [f In 1474.]
[g i.e., the other kings: Charles VIII and Louis XII.
[h M. alludes to the French having been forced out of Italy in 1512.]

foresight that they initiate policies that seem attractive, without noticing any poison that is concealed,[a] as I said earlier,[b] when referring to consumptive fevers.

Therefore, a ruler who does not recognise evils in the very early stages cannot be considered wise; this ability is given only to a few. If the beginning of the decline of the Roman Empire is sought, it will be found that it began only when the Goths started to be used as mercenaries,[c] because that policy began to sap the strength of the Roman Empire; and all the vigour that was drained from it was received by the Goths.

I conclude, then, that any principality that does not have its own army cannot be secure; rather, it must rely completely on luck or the favour of others, because it lacks the strength to defend itself in difficult times. Wise men have always thought and held 'quod nihil sit tam infirmum aut instabile quam fama potentiae non sua vi nixa'.[d] And one's own forces are those composed of subjects or citizens or of one's dependents; all the others are either mercenaries or auxiliaries. The right way to organise one's forces will be easily grasped, if the methods used by the four men I have cited above[e] are examined, and if it is understood how Philip, father of Alexander the Great, and many other republics and rulers have armed and organised their states; I have complete faith in their methods.

CHAPTER XIV

How a ruler should act concerning military matters

A ruler, then, should have no other objective and no other concern, nor

[a I.e., any underlying defects.]   [b See p. 11.]
[c By the Emperors Valens, in 376, and Theodosius the Great, in 382.]
[d Tacitus, *Annals*, XIII, 19: 'that nothing is so weak or unstable as a reputation for power that is not based on one's own forces'. This phrase differs slightly from what Tacitus wrote.]
[e I.e., Cesare Borgia, Hiero, Charles VII and David.]

occupy himself with anything else except war and its methods and practices, for this pertains only to those who rule. And it is of such efficacy that it not only maintains hereditary rulers in power but very often enables men of private status to become rulers. On the other hand, it is evident that if rulers concern themselves more with the refinements of life than with military matters, they lose power. The main reason why they lose it is their neglect of the art of war; and being proficient in this art is what enables one to gain power.

Because Francesco Sforza was armed, from being a private citizen he became Duke of Milan; since his descendants*a* did not trouble themselves with military matters, from being dukes they became private citizens. For being unarmed (apart from other bad consequences) results in your being despised, which is one of those disgraceful things against which a ruler must always guard, as will be explained later.*b* There is an enormous difference between an armed and an unarmed man; and it cannot be expected that a man who is armed will obey willingly a man who is unarmed, or that an unarmed man can be safe among armed servants.*c* Since the latter will be contemptuous and the former suspicious and afraid, they will not be able to work well together. Therefore, apart from the other disadvantages already mentioned, a ruler who does not understand military matters cannot be highly regarded by his soldiers, and he cannot trust them.

A ruler should therefore always be concerned with military matters, and in peacetime he should be even more taken up with them than in war. There are two ways of doing this: one is by going on exercises; the other is by study.*d*

With regard to exercises, besides keeping his troops well disciplined and trained, he should very frequently engage in hunting,*e* thus hardening his body and, at the same time, becoming familiar with the terrain: how mountains rise, how valleys open out and plains spread out,

---

[*a* *figliuoli*, which normally means 'sons'. Probably a reference to Ludovico, who lost his state and became a 'private citizen' (indeed, a prisoner of the French) in 1500, and also to his son, Massimiliano, who became Duke of Milan in 1512, and lost power in Sept. 1515; if so, the plural form would be a later interpolation by M., since *The Prince* was almost certainly completed no later than mid-1514.]

[*b* Esp. in Ch. XIX.]

[*c* *servitori armati*: i.e., soldiers, as is made clear at the end of this paragraph.]

[*d* *con la mente*: i.e., studying historical works that deal with war.]

[*e* Cf. *Disc.* III, 39.]

as well as with the characteristics of rivers and swamps; he should concern himself very much with all these matters.

This practical knowledge is valuable in two ways. First, one learns well the terrain of one's own country, and understands better its natural defences; secondly, through knowing and exercising in the countryside, one easily grasps the characteristics of any new terrain that must be explored. For the hills, valleys, plains, rivers and swamps that are found in Tuscany, for instance, are in many respects similar to those found in other regions. Thus, knowing well the terrain of one region readily permits one to become familiar with that of other regions. A ruler who lacks such expertise lacks the elements of generalship. For it enables one to track down the enemy, to encamp one's army properly, to lead an army towards the enemy, to prepare for battle, to besiege fortresses or fortified towns, in ways that conduce to victory.

One of the reasons why historians[a] have praised Philopoemen, the leader of the Achaean League, is that in peacetime he was always thinking about military matters; and when he was in the countryside with companions, he often stopped and asked questions: 'If the enemy happened to be up on that hill, and we were here with our army, who would be better placed? How should we attack them, while still preserving proper military formation? How should we be able to retreat? If they retreated, how should we pursue them?' As they travelled he used to put to them all the situations in which an army might be placed. He used to listen to their opinions, then give his own, supporting them with reasons. Because of these continual discussions, when he was leading his armies he was able to overcome any difficulties.

As for mental exercise, a ruler should read historical works, especially for the light they shed on the actions of eminent men: to find out how they waged war, to discover the reasons for their victories and defeats, in order to avoid reverses and achieve conquests; and above all, to imitate some eminent man, who himself set out to imitate some predecessor of his who was considered worthy of praise and glory, always taking his deeds and actions as a model for himself, as it is said[b] that Alexander the Great imitated Achilles, Caesar imitated Alexander, and Scipio imitated Cyrus. And anyone who reads the life of Cyrus,

[a Here M. follows Livy (XXV, 28), but presents the material more dramatically.]
[b Burd lists Plutarch, *Vita Alexandri*, VIII; Q. Curtius, *Historiarum Alexandri libri*, IV, 6; Suetonius, *Divus Julius*, 7; Cicero, *Ad Quintum fratrem*, i, I, 8, 23.]

written by Xenophon,[a] will realise, when he considers Scipio's life and career, how greatly Scipio's imitation of Cyrus helped him to attain glory, and how much Scipio's sexual restraint,[b] affability, humanity and generosity derived from his imitating the qualities of Cyrus, as recorded in this work by Xenophon. A wise ruler should act in such ways, and never remain idle in quiet times, but assiduously strengthen his position through such activities[c] in order that in adversity he will benefit from them. Thus, when his situation worsens, he will be well equipped to overcome dangers and to flourish.

CHAPTER XV

The things for which men, and especially rulers, are praised or blamed

It remains now to consider in what ways a ruler should act with regard to his subjects and allies.[d] And since I am well aware that many people have written about this subject I fear that I may be thought presumptuous, for what I have to say differs from the precepts offered by others, especially on this matter. But because I want to write what will be useful to anyone who understands, it seems to me better to concentrate on what really happens rather than on theories or speculations. For many have imagined republics and principalities that have never been seen or known to exist.[e] However, how men live is so different from how they should live that a ruler who does not do what is generally done, but persists in doing what ought to be done, will undermine his power rather than maintain it. If a ruler who wants always to act honourably is surrounded by many unscrupulous men his downfall is inevitable.

[a *Cyropaedia.*]   [b An instance of Scipio's sexual restraint is given in *Disc.* III, 20.]
[c I.e., keeping the army well trained and prepared for war, hunting and observing the terrain, and profiting from reading about war in historical books.]
[d A ruler's conduct towards subjects is treated in Chs. XV–XVII, towards allies (*amici*) in Ch. XVIII.]
[e M. apparently refers both to some ancient writers (e.g., Plato, in his *Republic*) and to more recent ones who emphasised ideals and the duties of rulers.]

Therefore, a ruler who wishes to maintain his power must be prepared[a] to act immorally when this becomes necessary.

I shall set aside fantasies about rulers, then, and consider what happens in fact. I say that whenever men are discussed, and especially rulers (because they occupy more exalted positions), they are praised or blamed for possessing some of the following qualities. Thus, one man is considered generous, another miserly (I use this Tuscan term[b] because *avaro* in our tongue also signifies someone who is rapacious, whereas we call *misero* someone who is very reluctant to use his own possessions); one is considered a free giver, another rapacious; one cruel, another merciful; one treacherous, another loyal; one effeminate and weak, another indomitable and spirited; one affable, another haughty; one lascivious, another moderate; one upright, another cunning; one inflexible, another easy-going; one serious, another frivolous; one devout, another unbelieving, and so on.

I know that everyone will acknowledge that it would be most praiseworthy for a ruler to have all the above-mentioned qualities that are held to be good. But because it is not possible to have all of them, and because circumstances do not permit living a completely virtuous life, one must be sufficiently prudent to know how to avoid becoming notorious for those vices that would destroy one's power and seek to avoid those vices that are not politically dangerous; but if one cannot bring oneself to do this, they can be indulged in with fewer misgivings. Yet one should not be troubled about becoming notorious for those vices without which it is difficult to preserve one's power, because if one considers everything carefully, doing some things that seem virtuous may result in one's ruin, whereas doing other things that seem vicious may strengthen one's position and cause one to flourish.

CHAPTER XVI

Generosity and meanness

To begin, then, with the first of the above-mentioned qualities, I

[a] *imparare*, which some commentators think here means 'to learn'.]
[b] *misero*, which has only one sense when contrasted with *liberale* ('generous'); M. avoids using *avaro* because it is ambiguous.]

maintain that it would be desirable to be considered generous; never-theless, if generosity[a] is practised in such a way that you will be considered generous, it will harm you. If it is practised virtuously, and as it should be, it will not be known about, and you will not avoid acquiring a bad reputation for the opposite vice.[b] Therefore, if one wants to keep up a reputation for being generous, one must spend lavishly and ostentatiously. The inevitable outcome of acting in such ways is that the ruler will consume all his resources in sumptuous display; and if he wants to continue to be thought generous, he will eventually be compelled to become rapacious, to tax the people very heavily, and raise money by all possible means.[c] Thus, he will begin to be hated by his subjects and, because he is impoverished, he will be held in little regard. Since this generosity of his has harmed many people and benefited few, he will feel the effects of any discontent, and the first real threat to his power will involve him in grave difficulties. When he realises this, and changes his ways, he will very soon acquire a bad reputation for being miserly.

Therefore, since a ruler cannot both practise this virtue of generosity and be known to do so without harming himself, he would do well not to worry about being called miserly. For eventually he will come to be considered more generous,[d] when it is realised that, because of his parsimony, his revenues are sufficient to defend himself against any enemies that attack him, and to undertake campaigns without imposing special taxes on the people. Thus he will be acting generously towards the vast majority, whose property he does not touch, and will be acting meanly towards the few to whom he gives nothing.[e]

Those rulers who have achieved great things in our own times have all been considered mean; all the others have failed. Although Pope Julius II cultivated a reputation for generosity in order to become pope,[f] he did not seek to maintain it afterwards, because he wanted to be able to wage war. The present King of France[g] has fought many wars without imposing any special taxes on his subjects, because his parsi-

---

[a] *liberalità*; in M.'s works, *generosità* always denotes nobility of spirit or magnanimity, and it acquired the sense of 'generosity' only later in the sixteenth century.]
[b] I.e., *parsimonia*, 'meanness' or 'miserliness'.]
[c] Cf. Cicero, *De officiis*, II, 15.]
[d] Clearly, in a different sense of the word; a 'genuine' generosity.]
[e] I.e., courtiers and others who would have expected to benefit from a 'generous' ruler.]
[f] I.e., by bribes.]   [g] Louis XII.]

monious habits have always enabled him to meet the extra expenses. If the present King of Spain[a] had a reputation for generosity, he would not have successfully undertaken so many campaigns.

Therefore, a ruler should worry little about being thought miserly: he will not have to rob his subjects; he will be able to defend himself; he will avoid being poor and despised and will not be forced to become rapacious. For meanness is one of those vices that enable him to rule. It may be objected that Caesar obtained power through his open-handedness, and that many others have risen to very high office because they were open-handed and were considered to be so. I would reply that either you are already an established ruler or you are trying to become a ruler. In the first case, open-handedness is harmful; in the second, it is certainly necessary to be thought open-handed. Caesar was one of those who sought power in Rome; but if after gaining power he had survived,[b] and had not moderated his expenditure, he would have undermined his power. And if it should be objected that many rulers who have been considered very generous have had remarkable military successes, I would reply: a ruler spends either what belongs to him or his subjects,[c] or what belongs to others. In the former case, he should be parsimonious; in the latter, he should be as open-handed as possible. A ruler who accompanies his army, supporting it by looting, sacking and extortions, disposes of what belongs to others; he must be open-handed, for if he is not, his soldiers will desert. You can be much more generous with what does not belong to you or to your subjects, as Cyrus, Caesar and Alexander were. This is because giving away what belongs to others in no way damages your reputation; rather, it enhances it.[d] It is only giving away what belongs to yourself that harms you.

There is nothing that is so self-consuming as generosity: the more you practise it, the less you will be able to continue to practise it.[e] You will either become poor and despised or your efforts to avoid poverty will make you rapacious and hated. A ruler must above all guard against being despised and hated; and being generous will lead to both. Therefore, it is shrewder to cultivate a reputation for meanness, which

[a Ferdinand the Catholic.]   [b I.e., if he had not been assassinated.]
[c Here M. blurs the distinction between the ruler's property and his subjects' property.]
[d M. obviously meant: in the eyes of his subjects or soldiers.]
[e Cf. Cicero, *De officiis*, II, 15, 52.]

will lead to notoriety but not to hatred. This is better than being forced, through wanting to be considered generous, to incur a reputation for rapacity, which will lead to notoriety and to hatred as well.

CHAPTER XVII

Cruelty and mercifulness; and whether it is better to be loved or feared

Turning to the other previously mentioned qualities,[a] I maintain that every ruler should want to be thought merciful, not cruel; nevertheless, one should take care not to be merciful in an inappropriate way. Cesare Borgia was considered cruel, yet his harsh measures restored order to the Romagna, unifying it and rendering it peaceful and loyal.[b] If his conduct is properly considered, he will be judged to have been much more merciful than the Florentine people, who let Pistoia be torn apart, in order to avoid acquiring a reputation for cruelty. Therefore, if a ruler can keep his subjects united and loyal, he should not worry about incurring a reputation for cruelty; for by punishing a very few he will really be more merciful than those who over-indulgently permit disorders to develop, with resultant killings and plunderings. For the latter usually harm a whole community, whereas the executions ordered by a ruler harm only specific individuals. And a new ruler, in particular, cannot avoid being considered harsh, since new states are full of dangers. Virgil makes Dido say:

> Res dura, et regni novitas me talia cogunt
> moliri, et late fines custode tueri.[d]

Nevertheless, he should be slow to believe accusations and to act against individuals, and should not be afraid of his own shadow. He

[a See p. 55.] [b See pp. 25–6.]

[c M. refers to events in late 1501, when the Panciatichi and Cancellieri factions were fighting each other. See *Disc.* III, 27.]

[d Virgil, *Aeneid*, I, 563–4: 'Harsh necessity and the newness of my kingdom force me to do such things, and to guard all the frontiers.']

should act with due prudence and humanity so that being over-confident will not make him incautious, and being too suspicious will not render him insupportable.

A controversy has arisen about this: whether it is better to be loved than feared, or vice versa.[a] My view is that it is desirable to be both loved and feared; but it is difficult to achieve both and, if one of them has to be lacking, it is much safer to be feared than loved.

For this may be said of men generally: they are ungrateful, fickle, feigners and dissemblers, avoiders of danger, eager for gain. While you benefit them they are all devoted to you: they would shed their blood for you; they offer their possessions, their lives, and their sons, as I said before,[b] when the need to do so is far off. But when you are hard pressed, they turn away. A ruler who has relied completely on their promises, and has neglected to prepare other defences, will be ruined, because friendships that are acquired with money, and not through greatness and nobility of character, are paid for but not secured, and prove unreliable just when they are needed.

Men are less hesitant about offending or harming a ruler who makes himself loved than one who inspires fear. For love is sustained by a bond of gratitude which, because men are excessively self-interested,[c] is broken whenever they see a chance to benefit themselves. But fear is sustained by a dread of punishment that is always effective. Nevertheless, a ruler must make himself feared in such a way that, even if he does not become loved, he does not become hated. For it is perfectly possible to be feared without incurring hatred. And this can always be achieved if he refrains from laying hands on the property of his citizens and subjects, and on their womenfolk.[d] If it is necessary to execute anyone, this should be done only if there is a proper justification and obvious reason. But, above all, he must not touch the property of others, because men forget sooner the killing[e] of a father than the loss of their patrimony.[f] Moreover, there will always be pretexts for seizing property; and someone who begins to live rapaciously will always find

---

[a See A. Gilbert, *Machiavelli's 'Prince' and its Forerunners*, pp. 103–15.]

[b See p. 37.]

[c *tristi*; its usual meaning is 'bad', but in some contexts it has a different sense.]

[d These are persistent themes in M.'s works: e.g., pp. 63–4; *Disc.* III, 6 (beg.), III, 26.]

[e *morte*: lit., 'death'.]

[f In an almost contemporary piece, M. says that everyone knows that a change of regime will not bring relatives back to life, but it could well result in one's property being restored.]

pretexts for taking the property of others. On the other hand, reasons or pretexts for taking life are rarer and more fleeting.

However, when a ruler is with his army, and commands a large force, he must not worry about being considered harsh, because armies are never kept united and prepared for military action unless their leader is thought to be harsh. Among the remarkable things recounted about Hannibal is that, although he had a very large army, composed of men from many countries,[a] and fighting in foreign lands,[b] there never arose any dissension, either among themselves or against their leader, whether things were going well or badly. This could be accounted for only by his inhuman cruelty which, together with his many good qualities, made him always respected and greatly feared by his troops. And if he had not been so cruel, his other qualities would not have been sufficient to achieve that effect. Thoughtless writers admire this achievement of his, yet condemn the main reason for it.

That his other qualities would not have sufficed is proved by what happened to Scipio, considered a most remarkable man not only in his own times but in all others, whose armies rebelled against him in Spain.[c] The only reason for this was that he was over-indulgent, and permitted his soldiers more freedom than was consistent with maintaining proper military discipline. Fabius Maximus rebuked him for this in the senate, and called him a corrupter of the Roman army. And when Locri[d] was ravaged by one of Scipio's legates, the inhabitants were not avenged by him, and the legate was not punished for his arrogance, all because Scipio was too easy-going. Indeed, a speaker in the senate who wished to excuse him said that there were many men who were better at not committing misdeeds themselves than punishing the misdeeds of others. This character of his would eventually have tarnished his fame and glory, if he had continued his military command unchecked; but since he was controlled by the senate, this harmful quality was not only concealed but contributed to his glory.

Returning to the matter of being feared and loved, then, I conclude that whether men bear affection depends on themselves, but whether

---

[a I.e., mercenaries.]

[b Far from home, and therefore subjected to particular stresses.]

[c In 206 B.C. See Livy, XXVIII, 24–5. There is a fuller comparison of Hannibal and Scipio in *Disc.* III, 21.]

[d Locri Epizephyrii was a Greek city in Calabria. For these events, see Livy, XXIX, 8–9, 16–22.]

they are afraid will depend on what the ruler does. A wise ruler should rely on what is under his own control, not on what is under the control of others; he should contrive only to avoid incurring hatred, as I have said.

CHAPTER XVIII

How rulers should keep their promises

Everyone knows how praiseworthy it is for a ruler to keep his promises, and live uprightly and not by trickery. Nevertheless, experience shows that in our times the rulers who have done great things are those who have set little store by keeping their word, being skilful rather in cunningly deceiving men; they have got the better of those who have relied on being trustworthy.

You should know, then, that there are two ways of contending: one by using laws, the other, force. The first is appropriate for men, the second for animals; but because the former is often ineffective, one must have recourse to the latter.*ª* Therefore, a ruler must know well how to imitate beasts as well as employing properly human means. This policy was taught to rulers allegorically by ancient writers: they tell how Achilles and many other ancient rulers*ᵇ* were entrusted to Chiron the centaur, to be raised carefully by him. Having a mentor who was half-beast and half-man signifies that a ruler needs to use both natures, and that one without the other is not effective.

Since a ruler, then, must know how to act like a beast, he should imitate both the fox and the lion, for the lion is liable to be trapped, whereas the fox cannot ward off wolves. One needs, then, to be a fox to recognise traps, and a lion to frighten away wolves. Those who rely merely upon a lion's strength do not understand matters.*ᶜ*

Therefore, a prudent ruler cannot keep his word, nor should he, when such fidelity would damage him, and when the reasons that made

[*ª* See pp. xix–xx.] [*ᵇ* Hercules, Theseus, Aesculapius and Jason.]

[*ᶜ* It is implied that relying only on cunning is not a common error. See also *Disc.* II, 13.]

61

him promise are no longer relevant. This advice would not be sound if all men were upright; but because they are treacherous and would not keep their promises to you, you should not consider yourself bound to keep your promises to them.

Moreover, plausible reasons can always be found for such failure to keep promises. One could give countless modern examples of this, and show how many peace treaties and promises have been rendered null and void by the faithlessness of rulers; and those best able to imitate the fox have succeeded best. But foxiness should be well concealed: one must be a great feigner and dissembler. And men are so naive, and so much dominated by immediate needs, that a skilful deceiver always finds plenty of people who will let themselves be deceived.

I must mention one recent case: Alexander VI was concerned only with deceiving men, and he always found them gullible. No man ever affirmed anything more forcefully or with stronger oaths but kept his word less. Nevertheless, his deceptions were always effective, because he well understood the naivety of men.

A ruler, then, need not actually possess all the above-mentioned qualities,[a] but he must certainly seem to. Indeed, I shall be so bold as to say that having and always cultivating them is harmful, whereas seeming to have them is useful; for instance, to seem merciful, trustworthy, humane, upright and devout, and also to be so. But if it becomes necessary to refrain, you must be prepared to act in the opposite way, and be capable of doing it. And it must be understood that a ruler, and especially a new ruler, cannot always act in ways that are considered good because, in order to maintain his power,[b] he is often forced to act treacherously, ruthlessly or inhumanely, and disregard the precepts of religion. Hence, he must be prepared to vary his conduct as the winds of fortune and changing circumstances constrain him and, as I said before,[c] not deviate from right conduct if possible, but be capable of entering upon the path of wrongdoing when this becomes necessary.

A ruler, then, should be very careful that everything he says is replete with the five above-named qualities: to those who see and hear him, he should seem to be exceptionally merciful, trustworthy, upright, humane and devout. And it is most necessary of all to seem devout. In

[a Those classified as good on p. 55.]
[b *per mantenere lo stato: stato* certainly signifies 'power' or 'government', though M. may be referring also to the political community. Cf. p. 63 n. *b*.]
[c Earlier in this paragraph, and on p. 55.]

these matters, most men judge more by their eyes than by their hands. For everyone is capable of seeing you, but few can touch you. Everyone can see what you appear to be, whereas few have direct experience of what you really are;[a] and those few will not dare to challenge the popular view, sustained as it is by the majesty of the ruler's position. With regard to all human actions, and especially those of rulers, who cannot be called to account, men pay attention to the outcome. If a ruler, then, contrives to conquer, and to preserve the state,[b] the means will always be judged to be honourable and be praised by everyone. For the common people are impressed by appearances and results.[c] Everywhere the common people are the vast majority, and the few[d] are isolated when the majority and the government are at one. One present-day ruler, whom it is well to leave unnamed,[e] is always preaching peace and trust, although he is really very hostile to both; and if he had practised them he would have lost either reputation or power several times over.

CHAPTER XIX

How contempt and hatred should be avoided

Since I have already discussed the most important of the qualities previously mentioned,[f] I want to discuss the others briefly under this general heading: that a ruler, as has already been partly explained,[g] should avoid anything that will make him either hated or despised. If he does avoid this he will have done what he should, and none of his other censurable faults will involve him in any danger.

What will make him hated, above all else, as I said,[h] is being

---

[a Lit., 'few touch that which you are'.]

[b *mantenere lo stato*: the context seems to imply that *stato* signifies 'political community', not just the 'government'.]

[c Strictly speaking, it would be the *apparent* outcomes. On the theme of appearance and reality, see *Disc.* I, 25, I, 47, I, 53; on judging by the outcome, see *Disc.* III, 35.]

[d I.e., the discerning few, those who experience the realities of power, who do not only 'see', who are not taken in by appearances.]

[e Ferdinand the Catholic (d. 1516); for his methods, see pp. 76–7.]

[f See p. 55.]   [g In Chs. XVI and XVII.]   [h See p. 59.]

rapacious and seizing the property or womenfolk of his subjects: he must avoid doing these things. If the vast majority of men are not deprived of their property and honour[a] they will live contentedly, and one will have to deal only with the ambition of a few men, which can easily be restrained in various ways.

What will make him despised is being considered inconstant, frivolous, effeminate, pusillanimous and irresolute: a ruler must avoid contempt as if it were a reef. He should contrive that his actions should display grandeur, courage, seriousness and strength, and his decisions about the private disputes of his subjects should be irrevocable. He should maintain this reputation, so that no one should think of lying to him or scheming to trick him.

A ruler who succeeds in creating such an image of himself will enjoy a fine reputation; and it will be difficult to plot against or to attack him (provided that he is known to be very able, and greatly respected and feared by his subjects). For rulers should have two main worries: one is internal, and concerns his subjects; the other is external, and concerns foreign powers. Against the latter threat, good troops and reliable allies are an effective defence; and possessing good armies always results in having allies who are reliable. If external relations are solidly based, internal affairs will give no trouble unless they have already been disturbed by conspiracy. Even if there are external threats, provided the ruler lives and arranges his affairs as I have recommended, and is not faint-hearted, he will always be able to repel any attacks, just as Nabis the Spartan did, as I mentioned earlier.[b]

But with regard to one's subjects, if there is no external threat, one's only fear must be that they may be plotting secretly. A ruler will effectively protect himself from this danger if he avoids incurring hatred and contempt, and keeps the people satisfied with him. It is essential to do this, as I said at length earlier.[c] One of the best safeguards that a ruler has against plots[d] is not being hated by the people. For plotters always believe that killing a ruler will satisfy the people. But if plotters think that the people will be angry, they will be

---

[a See p. 59 n. *d*. Offences against women are conceived of by M. primarily as dishonouring their menfolk; the offence against the women themselves is not emphasised.]
[b See p. 36.]　　[c See pp. 36–7, and also p. 59.]
[d This topic is dealt with at great length in *Disc.* III, 6.]

most reluctant to undertake a conspiracy, because it always involves countless difficulties and dangers for them. There have been many conspiracies, but history has shown that few have succeeded. For a conspirator cannot act alone; yet he cannot seek help except from those whom he believes to be disaffected. But as soon as you have revealed your plan to a malcontent, you enable him to become contented, because obviously he can now expect to be amply rewarded.[a] If he sees that there is certain gain to be had in this way, and only many dangers and uncertain gain from joining the plot, he must either be an exceptional friend or an implacable enemy of the ruler, if he fails to give you away. In short, for plotters there are only fears of discovery or betrayal, and the dreadful prospect of punishment; but the ruler has the prestige attaching to his office, together with the laws and resources of government at his disposal, as well as help from allies, all of which will help him to survive. It follows that, if popular goodwill is added to all these other advantages, only an exceedingly rash man would dare to conspire against him. Plotters normally have grounds for being afraid before the crime is carried out; but here what has to be feared as well is that afterwards, when the deed has been done, the people will be hostile and there will be no hope of being given refuge by them.

Countless examples could be given on this subject; but I shall limit myself to one, which occurred in our fathers' time. Messer Annibale Bentivoglio, grandfather of the present messer Annibale, who was ruler of Bologna, was conspired against and killed by the Canneschi family.[b] His only son was messer Giovanni, who was a babe in arms. Immediately after this killing, the people rose up and slaughtered all the Canneschi. The reason for this was the popular goodwill towards the Bentivoglio at that time, which was very great. After Annibale's death, no member of the family was left in Bologna[c] who could govern that state. When it was heard from Florence that one of the Bentivoglio family[d] (until then believed to be a blacksmith's son) was living there, the Bolognese came to Florence to find him and entrusted the government of that city to him; and he governed it until Giovanni was old enough to rule.

[a By the ruler, for denouncing the plot.] [b In 1445. See p. 118.]
[c Giovanni Bentivoglio was far too young.]
[d Sante Bentivoglio, probably an illegitimate son of Ercole Bentivoglio, cousin of Annibale I.]

I conclude, then, that rulers should worry little about being plotted against if their subjects are well disposed towards them, but if their subjects are hostile and hate them, they should be afraid of everything and everyone. Well-ordered states and wise rulers have always been very careful not to exasperate the nobles and also to satisfy the people and keep them contented; this is one of the most important things for a ruler to do.

France is one of the best-ordered and best-governed modern kingdoms; and in that country there are countless good institutions, on which the liberty and security of the king is based. The most important of these is the *parlement*, which possesses great authority. For the man who reformed that kingdom[a] was well aware of the ambition and arrogance of the nobles, and thought that they needed a bit in their mouths to restrain them. On the other hand, since he knew that the people hated the nobles because they were afraid of them, he wanted to protect the people. He did not want this restraint to be a special duty of the king, in order not to make him hated by the nobles because he favoured the people, and not to make him hated by the people because he favoured the nobles. Consequently, he set up another body[b] to restrain the nobles and favour the people, without the king having to incur any hostility. There could have been no more prudent measure or better institution than this, or anything that has strengthened more the monarchy and the kingdom itself. Another important lesson can be learned from this: rulers should leave unpleasant tasks to others, but themselves do those things that increase their popularity. Again, I would emphasise that a ruler should respect the nobles, but not act in a way that makes the people hate him.

It will perhaps seem to many people that, if the lives, careers and deaths of some of the Roman emperors are examined, they will provide evidence against the views I have expressed. For some emperors always lived admirable lives and displayed greatness of spirit, yet either lost power or were killed by their soldiers or courtiers, who plotted against them. I want to reply to these objections, then, consider the characters of some emperors and show the reasons why they failed (which are not inconsistent with what I have maintained). I also want to emphasise those things that are important for anyone who studies the deeds done in those times.

[a A reference to Louis IX, who apparently instituted the *parlement* of Paris about 1254; his grandson, Philip the Fair, clarified and defined its functions.]
[b The *parlement* of Paris.]

I want to limit my survey to the emperors who ruled from Marcus the philosopher[a] until Maximinus: namely, Marcus, his son Commodus, Pertinax, Julianus, Severus,[b] his son Antoninus Caracalla, Macrinus, Heliogabalus, Alexander[c] and Maximinus. The first point that should be made is that, whereas in other principalities only the ambition of the nobles and the insolence of the people had to be reckoned with, the Roman emperors were confronted by a third problem: they had to deal with the cruelty and rapacity of the soldiers. This was such a great problem that it caused the downfall of many emperors. For it was hard to satisfy both the soldiers and the people: the reason was that the people liked a peaceful life, and consequently wanted to have moderate rulers, whereas the soldiers wanted warlike rulers, who were arrogant, cruel and rapacious. The soldiers wanted the people to be treated harshly by rulers, so that they could have double pay[d] and give vent to their own rapacity and cruelty.

The outcome was that those emperors who (either through natural deficiencies or lack of experience) did not acquire sufficient prestige to be able to restrain both the soldiers and the people always failed. And most of the emperors (especially those who came to the throne as new men), when they realised how difficult it was to satisfy these two conflicting tendencies, tried to satisfy the soldiers and worried little about the people being harmed.

They were forced to follow this policy. Since rulers cannot avoid being hated in some quarters, the first thing they should do is to try not to be hated by everyone; and if this cannot be achieved, to strive assiduously to avoid the hatred of the groups that are most powerful.

Consequently, the emperors who stood specially in need of support (because they were new rulers) favoured the soldiers rather than the people. However, whether this profited them or not depended on whether they were capable of keeping the respect of the soldiers.

Marcus, Pertinax and Alexander, who all lived moderately, who loved justice and shunned cruelty, who were all humane and benevolent, came (apart from Marcus) to a bad end. Only Marcus lived and died honoured by all, because he became emperor by hereditary right, and did not owe his power either to the soldiers or to the people. Then,

---

[a Marcus Aurelius; the period covered is A.D. 161–238. M.'s source was Herodian's history, which he follows closely; it was translated into Latin by Poliziano in 1493.]
[b Septimius Severus.]   [c Alexander Severus.]
[d To receive booty as well as their normal pay.]

because he had many fine qualities, which made him greatly respected, throughout his reign he was able to keep both the soldiers and the people under control, and he always avoided being hated or despised.

But Pertinax was made emperor against the will of the soldiers who, being used to doing as they pleased under Commodus, could not bear to live properly, as Pertinax wanted them to do. Thus he became hated and, since he was despised as well (because he was old), he was slain soon after the start of his reign.

It should be remarked at this point that good deeds as well as bad may incur hatred. As I said earlier,[a] a ruler who wants to maintain his power is often forced to act immorally. For if a group (whether it is the people or the soldiers or the nobles) whose support you consider necessary for maintaining your power is corrupt, you are forced to indulge its proclivities in order to satisfy it. In such circumstances, good deeds are inimical to you.

But let us come to Alexander, whose rectitude was so notable that he was praised for many things. One of them was the fact that, during the fourteen years that he held power, he never had anyone executed without a trial. Nevertheless, because he was considered weak, and a man who allowed himself to be controlled by his mother,[b] he came to be despised, the army plotted against him and he was killed.

Let us now consider, by contrast, the characters of Commodus, Severus, Antoninus Caracalla and Maximinus: they were all exceedingly cruel and rapacious. In order to satisfy the soldiers, they did not hesitate to commit every kind of injury against the people; and all of them, except Severus, came to a bad end.

Severus possessed so much ability that he was able to keep the soldiers friendly, and rule successfully to the end, even though he oppressed the people. For his outstanding qualities made him so remarkable in the eyes of the soldiers and the people that the latter were astonished and awestruck, while the former were respectful and satisfied. For a new ruler, the deeds of this man were very impressive, so I want to show briefly how well he was able to imitate the fox and the lion, which I said earlier was necessary for a ruler to do.[c] Severus was well aware of the indolence of the Emperor Julianus, and he persuaded the army he commanded in Slavonia[d] that it would be a good idea to march

[a See pp. 55, 62.]   [b Julia Avita Mamaea.]
[c See pp. 61–2.]   [d Illyria.]

on Rome, and avenge the death of Pertinax, who had been killed by his praetorian guard. Using this pretext, without revealing that he wanted to become emperor, he took his army towards Rome with such speed that he reached Italy before it was known he had left Slavonia. When he arrived in Rome, the intimidated senate elected him emperor, and had Julianus killed. After this beginning, two difficulties remained to be overcome before Severus could control the whole Empire. One was in Asia, where Nigrinus, leader of the Asian armies, had been proclaimed emperor; the other was in the west, where Albinus also aspired to the imperial throne. Since Severus thought it would be dangerous to reveal his hostility to both men, he decided to attack only Nigrinus and to trick Albinus. Accordingly, he wrote to Albinus, saying that the senate had chosen him emperor, and that he wanted to share the office. And he sent Albinus the title of Caesar, saying that by decision of the senate Albinus should join him as co-emperor. Albinus thought all this was true. But when Severus had defeated and killed Nigrinus, and the eastern part of the Empire was calm, he returned to Rome and complained to the senate that Albinus, showing little gratitude for the benefits he had received, had treacherously attempted to kill him, and that it was therefore necessary to go and punish his ingratitude. Then Severus attacked Albinus in France, where he deprived him at once of his position and his life.

If Severus's deeds are examined closely, it must be concluded that he was a very fierce lion and a very cunning fox, who was feared and respected by everyone, and was not hated by his soldiers. And it should not be a matter of surprise that he, a new ruler, was able to rule such a great empire: for his immense prestige always protected him from the hatred that the people might have had for him because of his rapacious deeds.

His son Antoninus was also a man with many very fine qualities, who was greatly admired by the people and liked by the soldiers. For he was a hardened warrior, who despised delicate food and any kind of weakness; this endeared him to all his soldiers. Nevertheless, he committed very many deeds of unexampled barbarity and cruelty: countless individuals were killed, as well as most of the inhabitants of Rome and all those of Alexandria. As a result, he became greatly hated by everyone. Even those around him began to be afraid of him, and one day he was killed by a centurion in the midst of his own troops.

Here it should be remarked that such assassinations, which result from the resolve of implacable enemies, cannot be guarded against by rulers, because anyone who does not fear death himself can kill a ruler. But since this happens very rarely, a ruler should be much less afraid of it. He should be careful only not to harm seriously or insult anyone who serves him or any courtiers, as Antoninus did: he had outrageously put to death a brother of that centurion, and had continually threatened the centurion himself; yet he kept the man in his bodyguard. This was a rash decision and likely to cause his downfall, as indeed happened.

But let us consider Commodus, who should have found it very easy to retain power, since he had inherited it from his father Marcus. He needed only to follow in the footsteps of his father, and he would have satisfied both the soldiers and the people. But because he was naturally cruel and brutal, he began to curry favour with the soldiers and let them behave as they liked so as to satisfy his rapacity at the people's expense. Moreover, he was not careful to uphold his dignity, for he often went down into the theatres to fight with the gladiators; as he did other things that were very degrading, and not in keeping with his imperial rank, he became despised by the soldiers. Since he was hated by the people and despised by the soldiers, he was conspired against and killed.

It remains to discuss the character of Maximinus. He was an extremely warlike man; and since the soldiers had greatly disliked the unmanly conduct of Alexander (whom I have mentioned earlier),[a] after he had been killed the soldiers chose Maximinus as emperor. But he did not retain power for very long, because two things made him hated and despised. One was that he was of very low birth: he had been a shepherd in Thrace (this was well known to everybody and caused him to be greatly despised). The other was that, at the beginning of his rule, he had put off going to Rome and taking possession of the imperial throne. This delay earned him a reputation for being cruel, because his prefects, carrying out his orders, had committed many cruel acts, both in Rome and in many other parts of the Empire. The result was that, since everyone was outraged by his low birth and filled with hatred, and because they were afraid of his brutality, first Africa revolted, then the senate and all the people of Rome; then the rest of Italy rose up against him. Finally, his own army rebelled: his troops were besieging Aquileia, which they found a difficult operation; they became angry at his harshness, and taking courage from knowing that so many had turned against him, they killed him.

[a See p. 68.]

I do not wish to discuss Heliogabalus, Macrinus or Julianus: because they were generally despised, they were soon killed. I want to bring this survey to a close. I maintain that the rulers of our own times are not troubled by the need to satisfy their soldiers by violent and illegal means. Although they have to pay some attention to them, any problems are quickly resolved, because none of these rulers has raised armies that are used to being together for long periods, controlling and administering provinces, as the armies of the Roman Empire did. Hence, if it was then more necessary to satisfy the soldiers than the people, it was because the soldiers were more powerful.

Nowadays, for all rulers, except the Sultans of Turkey and Egypt, it is more necessary to satisfy the people than the soldiers, because the people are now more powerful. The Sultan of Turkey is an exception because he always keeps twelve thousand foot-soldiers and fifteen thousand cavalry in his service near him,[a] and the security and strength of his Kingdom depends on these forces. Hence, he must keep these forces friendly, and pay more regard to them than to others. Likewise, since the Kingdom of the Sultan of Egypt is completely in the hands of the soldiers, he too is obliged to keep them friendly, without considering what the people may want. Moreover, it should be noted that this Sultan's state is different from every other principality. It resembles the Papacy (which cannot be called either an hereditary principality or a new principality): for it is not the sons of the old ruler who are the heirs, and then become rulers, but the man who is elected to that position by those who are authorised. Since this institution is ancient, it cannot be called a new principality, for it lacks all the problems encountered in new principalities. Although its ruler is certainly new, the institutions of the state are old, and are ready to receive him as if he were an hereditary ruler.

But let us return to our subject. I maintain that anyone who considers what I have written will realise that either hatred or contempt led to the downfall of the emperors I have discussed; he will recognise that some of them acted in one way and others in the opposite way, and that one ruler in each group was successful and the others ended badly. Because Pertinax and Alexander were new rulers, it was useless and harmful for them to act like Marcus, who was an hereditary ruler. Likewise, it was harmful for Caracalla, Commodus and Maximinus to act like Severus,

[a The janissaries.]

71

because they lacked the ability required to follow in his footsteps. Therefore, a new ruler in a new principality cannot imitate the conduct of Marcus, nor again is it necessary to imitate that of Severus. Rather, he should imitate Severus in the courses of action that are necessary for establishing himself in power, and imitate Marcus in those that are necessary for maintaining power that is already established and secure, thus achieving glory.

CHAPTER XX

Whether building fortresses, and many other things that rulers frequently do, are useful or not

To maintain their power more securely, some rulers have disarmed their subjects; others have encouraged factions in towns subject to them; others have fostered hostility against themselves; others have sought to win over those of whom they were suspicious when they began to rule; some have built fortresses and others have destroyed them. Although a definite judgement cannot be passed on all these measures, unless the particular circumstances of those states in which such decisions are taken are examined, nevertheless I shall discuss the subject in terms as general as it permits.

New rulers, then, never disarm their subjects; indeed, if they find them unarmed, they always provide them with weapons. For when you arm them, these weapons become your own: those whom you distrusted become loyal, those who were loyal remain so, and subjects are converted into firm adherents. Since it is not possible to provide all your subjects with arms, when you benefit those whom you arm, you will also be able to secure yourself better against the others. Since the former are treated favourably, they will be more attached to you. The latter will excuse your conduct, because they will realise the need to treat favourably those who carry out more dangerous duties.

But if you disarm your subjects, you begin to offend them, for you show that you do not trust them, either because you are weak and cowardly or because you are too suspicious. And both these reasons cause you to become hated. Since you cannot remain without military forces, you will be forced to resort to employing mercenary troops which will be of the stamp I have previously indicated.[a] And even if they happen to be effective, they cannot be sufficiently effective to defend you against powerful enemies and hostile subjects.

As I have said, then, new rulers of new principalities always arm their subjects. History is full of examples of this. But when a ruler annexes a state, which is joined like a member to his old one, he must then disarm the inhabitants of that state, except those who have helped him to annex it. However, in time, and as opportunity permits, even these must be rendered weak and harmless, and you must arrange matters so that all the arms of your enlarged state are in the hands of your own soldiers, who served under you in your old state.

Our ancestors, and those who were thought to be wise, used to say that it was necessary to hold Pistoia by means of the factions[b] and Pisa by using fortresses. Accordingly, they fostered discords between their subjects in some towns, so that they could maintain their hold on them more easily. This policy may have been sound in the period when there was a certain equilibrium in Italy;[c] but I do not think that it should be imitated today. My own view is that divisions never benefit anyone; on the contrary, when faction-ridden cities are threatened by an enemy force, they always fall very quickly. The reason is that the weaker faction always rallies to the invader, and the other is not strong enough to resist.

The Venetians used to foster the Guelph and Ghibelline factions[d] in their subject-cities (acting for the reasons mentioned above, I think); although they never permitted bloodshed, they were careful to foment discords among them, so that the citizens would be so absorbed in their quarrels that they would not unite against the Venetians. This policy did not profit them, as was seen: after their defeat at Vailà, some of these cities were immediately emboldened to revolt,[e] and they deprived the Venetians of all their land empire. The use of such methods, then,

[a] See Chs. XII and XIII.]   [b] See p. 58 n. *c*.]
[c] From the Peace of Lodi (1454) until 1494.]
[d] The Guelphs were the papal party, the Ghibellines the imperial party, in the medieval conflicts between the Papacy and the Empire. But in the early sixteenth century, the former term was used for supporters of Louis XII of France, and the latter for supporters of the Emperor Maximilian.]
[e] Brescia, Verona, Vicenza and Padua.]

indicates that a ruler is weak: such divisions are never permitted in a strong principality, for they are useful only in peacetime, when they can be used to control one's subjects more easily. But when war comes, the folly of such methods becomes apparent.

There is no doubt that rulers become great when they overcome difficulties and the attacks directed against them. For this reason fortune, especially when it wants to increase the power of a new ruler (who has more need to gain a reputation than an hereditary one) encourages the growth of enemies, and makes him fight against them, so that he will be able to vanquish them, and thus rise higher, as if by a ladder that his enemies have provided him with. Accordingly, many people consider that a shrewd ruler should seize any opportunity to encourage hostile forces cunningly, so that when he crushes them his reputation and power will be greatly increased.

Rulers (especially new rulers) have often found that men whom they had regarded with suspicion in the early stages of their rule prove more reliable and useful than those whom they had trusted at first. Pandolfo Petrucci, ruler of Siena, governed his state more with the help of those men of whom he had been suspicious than with anyone else. But it is very difficult to generalise about this, since men and circumstances vary. I shall say only that a ruler will always find it very easy to win over those men who were hostile to him in the early stages of his regime, but who were insufficiently powerful to maintain their position without help. For their part, they are constrained to serve him faithfully, because they are well aware how necessary it is for them to act in such a way as to cancel his initially unfavourable view of them. Thus, he will always find them more useful than those who, because they feel very secure in their positions, tend to neglect his affairs.

Moreover, since this matter is important, I do not want to fail to remind any ruler who has recently gained power through being favoured by the inhabitants[a] that he should be well aware of the reasons why those who helped him to gain power acted as they did. If it was not from natural affection for him, but only because they were discontented with the previous government, it will be very difficult and troublesome to keep them friendly, because he will not be able to satisfy them. Considering the reason for this (in the light of instances drawn from ancient and modern history), it is clear that it is much easier to win

[a See Chs. III and IX.]

74

over men who are hostile to him because they were content under the previous regime than it is to keep attached to him those who became friendly towards him and helped him to become ruler because they were disaffected.

Rulers have been accustomed to build fortresses[a] to strengthen their power. These serve as a bit and bridle for those who might plot against them, and are designed to provide a secure refuge if they should be subjected to a sudden attack. I praise this practice, because it has been used since ancient times. Nevertheless, in our own times, Niccolò Vitelli destroyed two fortresses in Città di Castello, so that he could maintain his rule over it.[b] Guido Ubaldo, Duke of Urbino, when he returned to his dominions, from which Cesare Borgia had driven him out,[c] razed to the ground all the fortresses of that region, because he considered that their destruction would make it less likely that he would lose power again. And when the Bentivoglio returned to power in Bologna[d] they followed the same policy.

Fortresses are sometimes useful, then, and sometimes not; it depends on the circumstances. Moreover, if they help you in some respects, they will be harmful in others. The subject may be clarified in the following way: if a ruler is more afraid of his own subjects than of foreigners, he should build fortresses; but a ruler who is more afraid of foreigners than of his own subjects should not build them. The castle of Milan, built by Francesco Sforza,[e] has been and will be a source of more trouble to the Sforza family than any other disorder of that state. Hence, the best fortress a ruler can have is not to be hated by the people: for if you possess fortresses and the people hate you, having fortresses will not save you, since if the people rise up there will never be any lack of foreign powers ready to help them. Fortresses have never been an advantage to any ruler of recent times, except the Countess of

[a Cf. *Disc.* II, 24.]
[b In 1482, when he returned there; he had been driven out in 1474 by Cardinal della Rovere (later Julius II), acting for Pope Sixtus IV.]
[c Guido Ubaldo Montefeltro; driven out of Urbino in June 1502, he returned in Oct. 1502, fled to Venice in Jan. 1503 (after the killings at Senigallia) and returned finally after Alexander VI's death in August 1503.]
[d The heirs of Giovanni Bentivoglio (who had been driven out of Bologna by Julius II in 1506) returned there in 1511, and destroyed the fortress that Julius had built at Porta Galliera.]
[e In 1450, as soon as he became ruler.]

Forlì,[a] when her husband Count Girolamo was assassinated.[b] For the fortress there provided her with a refuge from the popular uprising: she was able to await help from Milan[c] and then regain power. The circumstances were such that no foreign power was able to help the people. But fortresses were of little use to her later,[d] when Cesare Borgia attacked, and her hostile subjects rallied to the invading forces. Hence, on both occasions, not being hated by the people would have made her more secure than any fortresses did.

Bearing in mind all these things, then, I praise anyone who builds fortresses and anyone who does not, and I criticise anyone who relies upon fortresses, and does not worry about incurring the hatred of the people.

CHAPTER XXI

How a ruler should act in order to gain reputation

Nothing enables a ruler to gain more prestige than undertaking great campaigns and performing unusual deeds. In our own times Ferdinand of Aragon, the present King of Spain is a notable example. He might almost be called a new ruler because, from being a weak king,[e] he has become the most famous and glorious king in Christendom. And if his achievements are examined, they will all be found to be very remarkable, and some of them quite extraordinary. This man attacked Granada[f] at the beginning of his reign,[g] and this campaign laid the foundations of his state. First of all, he began this campaign when things were quiet and when he was not afraid of being opposed: he kept

[a Caterina Sforza Riario. See also *Disc.* III, 6.]
[b On 14 April 1488.]
[c From her uncle Ludovico il Moro, the virtual ruler.]
[d Caterina's subjects rebelled on 15 Dec. 1499, and she shut herself in the fortress; Cesare Borgia arrived at Forlì on 19 Dec.; on 28 Dec. he attacked the fortress, which fell on 12 Jan. 1500.]
[e When he was King only of Aragon, before becoming King of Castile in 1479.]
[f The Moorish kingdom in Southern Spain.]
[g In 1480. The conquest was completed in Jan. 1492.]

the minds of the barons of Castile occupied with that war, so that they would not plan any revolts. And he meanwhile was acquiring prestige, and increasing his hold over them before they were even aware of the fact. He was able to maintain armies with money from the Church[a] and from his subjects, and during that long war he was able to develop a powerful army, whose achievements have subsequently brought him so much honour. Moreover, in order to undertake even greater campaigns, he continued to make use of religion, resorting to a cruel and apparently pious policy of unexampled wretchedness: that of hunting down the Moors[b] and driving them out of his Kingdom. Using this same cloak,[c] he attacked Africa;[d] he invaded Italy;[e] and recently he has attacked France.[f] Thus he has always plotted and achieved great things, which have never failed to keep his subjects in a state of suspense and amazement, as they await their outcome. And these deeds of his have followed one another so quickly that nobody has had enough time to be able to initiate a revolt against him.

It is also very beneficial for a ruler to perform very unusual deeds within his kingdom, such as those recorded about messer Bernabò, the ruler of Milan.[g] When it happens that someone does something extraordinary (whether good or bad) in social or political life,[h] he should hit on some way of rewarding or punishing him that will be much talked about. Above all, a ruler must contrive to achieve through all his actions the reputation of being a great man of outstanding intelligence.

A ruler is also highly regarded if he is either a true ally or an outright enemy, that is, if he unhesitatingly supports one ruler against another. This policy is always better than remaining neutral, since if two powerful rulers near you come to blows, either the eventual victor will become a threat to you, or he will not. In either situation, it will always be wiser to intervene in favour of one side and fight strongly. For in the former situation, if you do not declare yourself, you will always be liable to be despoiled by the victor (which would please and satisfy the loser), and you will deservedly be defenceless and friendless. For the victor does

[a The war against this Moslem kingdom was seen as a crusade.]
[b In 1501–2. The Jews were also expelled.]
[c Using religion as a pretext.]
[d The African coast was occupied from Oran to Tripoli in 1509.]
[e The Kingdom of Naples was conquered in 1503. See pp. 5, 13, 14, 27.]
[f In 1512, for the possession of Navarre.]
[g Bernabò Visconti.]   [h *la vita civile*: everything that is not military.]

77

not want unreliable allies who did not help him when he was hard pressed; and the loser wil' not show you any favour, because you did not want to run the risk of sharing his fate by assisting him militarily.

Antiochus invaded Greece, invited there by the Aetolians in order to drive out the Romans.ª Antiochus sent envoys to the Achaeans, who were allies of the Romans, to advise them to remain neutral. On the other hand, the Romans exhorted them to take up arms on their behalf. This matter was discussed at a meeting of the Achaeans at which the envoy of Antiochus exhorted them to remain neutral. To this the Roman envoy replied: 'Quod autem isti dicunt non interponendi vos bello, nihil magis alienum rebus vestris est; sine gratia, sine dignitate, praemium victoris eritis.'ᵇ

A ruler who is not an ally will always want you to remain neutral, whereas one who is your ally will always want your armed support. In order to avoid present dangers, irresolute rulers usually prefer to remain neutral, and very often this is their undoing. However, let us assume that you strongly support one of the parties, who then emerges victorious: even if he is powerful and you are at his mercy, he is beholden to you and friendship is established between you. And men are never so dishonourable that they would attack you in such circumstances, and display so much ingratitude. Moreover, victories are never so decisive that the victor does not need to be careful, and especially about acting justly. But if the ruler whom you help loses, he will show gratitude to you and will help you as far as he can; thus you become an ally in a cause that may flourish again.

In the second situation (when the rulers fighting each other cannot be a threat to you), it is wiser still to intervene: because you will contribute to the downfall of one ruler, and are helped by another ruler who, if he had been wise, would have saved him;ᶜ and if together you win, the ruler whom you help will be at your mercy. (And it is certainly to be expected that he will overcome his enemy, since he has your help.)

[ª See p. 10.]
[ᵇ Livy, XXXV, 49: 'As for what they tell you, that it is better for you not to intervene in the war, nothing could be further from your interests; lacking help and dignity, you would be the prize of the victor.' The first part of the quotation is somewhat different from what Livy wrote.]
[ᶜ Instead of attacking him, for the reason given at the beginning of the next paragraph. (The hypothetical ruler being addressed by M. is more powerful than the two rulers in whose war he is advised to intervene.)]

Here it should be observed that a ruler should be careful never to ally himself with a ruler who is more powerful than himself in order to attack other powers, unless he is forced to, as has been said above. For if you are victorious together, you will be at his mercy, and rulers should do their best to avoid being at the mercy of other powers. The Venetians allied themselves with France against the Duke of Milan;[a] they could have avoided this alliance, and the outcome was their downfall. But if it is not possible to avoid such a commitment (as happened to the Florentines, when the Pope and the King of Spain launched an attack against Lombardy),[b] a ruler should then become involved for the reasons previously mentioned.

No government should ever believe that it is always possible to follow safe policies. Rather, it should be realised that all courses of action involve risks: for it is in the nature of things that when one tries to avoid one danger another is always encountered. But prudence consists in knowing how to assess the dangers, and to choose the least bad course of action as being the right one to follow.[c]

A ruler should also show himself a lover of talent,[d] and honour those who excel in any art. Moreover,[e] he should encourage the citizens to follow quietly their ordinary occupations, both in trade and agriculture and every other kind, so that one man is not afraid to improve or increase his possessions for fear that they will be taken from him, and another does not hesitate to begin to trade for fear of the taxes that will be levied. Rather, he should offer rewards to anyone who wants to do such things, and to anyone who seeks in any way to improve his city or country. Furthermore, at appropriate times of the year, he should keep the people entertained with feasts and spectacles. And since every city is divided into guilds or family groups he should pay due attention to these groups, meeting them from time to time, and performing acts that display his own affability and munificence. But he should always be careful to preserve the prestige of his office,[f] for this is something that should never be diminished.

[a Ludovico Sforza. See pp. 11, 12.]
[b In 1512.] [c Cf. *Disc.* I, 6.]
[d *virtú*, which here denotes primarily artistic and literary talents.]
[e The rest of this paragraph appears to owe something to Ch. 9 of Xenophon's *Hiero*.]
[f As some Roman emperors failed to do (see p. 70). Lorenzo the Magnificent was not always careful to preserve the dignity appropriate to his position (see *Ist. fior.* VIII, 36).]

CHAPTER XXII

The secretaries of rulers

The choosing of ministers*a* is a very important matter for a ruler: whether or not they are good depends on whether he is shrewd. The first indications of the intelligence of a ruler are given by the quality of the men around him. If they are capable and loyal, he should always be taken to be shrewd, because he was able to recognise their ability and retain their loyalty. But if they are mediocre and disloyal, a low estimate of him will never be mistaken, because the most important error he has made is to choose them.

Nobody who knew messer Antonio da Venafro*b* as minister of Pandolfo Petrucci, ruler of Siena, could fail to judge Pandolfo a very able man, just because he had Antonio as his minister. There are three kinds of mind: the first grasps things unaided; the second when they are explained; the third never understands at all. The first kind is exceptionally good, the second very good, the third useless. Consequently, even if Pandolfo did not belong to the first category, he certainly belonged to the second. For if a ruler shows judgement in discerning the worth of what another man says and does (even if he himself lacks originality of mind), he can discern the good or bad deeds of his minister, and reward the former but punish the latter. And since the minister realises that he cannot deceive his master, he is careful to behave well.

There is an infallible way for a ruler to weigh up a minister. If you realise that he is thinking more about his own affairs than about yours, and that all his actions are designed to further his own interests, he will never make a good minister, and you can never trust him. For a man who governs a state*c* should never think about himself or his own affairs but always about the ruler, and concern himself only with the ruler's affairs. On the other hand, in order to ensure the minister's fidelity, the ruler should look after him, by honouring him, enriching him, attach-

[*a* A *ministro* probably combines the duties of a 'minister' (in the modern sense) and a 'secretary'.]
[*b* Antonio Giordani da Venafro.]
[*c* *stato*: here it probably signifies primarily 'government'. It is spoken of almost as a personal possession (*lo stato d'uno*), 'belonging' to a *principe*, and entrusted, so to speak, to the *ministro*, or put in his hands (*in mano*).]

ing him to himself, conferring honours and offices on him; in short, treating the minister so that he will realise that he depends upon the ruler, and the many honours and riches will not make him want even more honours and riches, and his many offices will make him fear change.[a] If ministers and rulers have such a relationship, then, each will have confidence in the other; but if they do not, the outcome will always be that one or the other is harmed.

CHAPTER XXIII

How flatterers should be shunned

I do not want to leave undiscussed an important subject,[b] about which rulers easily make mistakes, unless they are very shrewd and are skilful at choosing men. I refer to flatterers, who are found everywhere in courts; for men are so wrapped up in their own affairs, in which they are so liable to make mistakes, that it is hard to defend oneself from this plague. Moreover, some ways of trying to protect oneself from flatterers involve the risk of becoming despised.

For the only way to protect yourself from flattery is by letting it be known that being told the truth does not offend you. However, if anyone may speak frankly to you, respect for you will soon disappear.

Therefore, a wise ruler will follow another way, and choose shrewd men for his service, permitting them alone to speak frankly, but only when he asks them and not otherwise. But he should ask them about everything, listen carefully to their views, and then make his own decisions. He should so conduct himself with his advisers that they will all realise that the more candidly they speak the more acceptable they will be. Apart from those he has chosen, he should refuse to listen to anyone, but pursue his aims steadfastly and not waver about decisions he has taken. Any ruler who does not act in this way either comes to

---

[a *le mutazioni*: a change of regime is implied.]
[b It was much discussed in Renaissance Europe: e.g., More, *A Dyalogue of Comforte Agaynste Tribulacyon*, III, 10; Erasmus, *Institutio principis christiani*, in *Opera omnia* (Amsterdam, 1974), vol. IV, 1, pp. 175–82; Castiglione, *Il Cortegiano*, II, 18; Elyot, *The Gouernor*, II, 14; Montaigne, *Essais*, III, 7; Bacon, *Essays*, XX, XXIII, XXVII.]

grief among flatterers or changes his decisions often because of the conflicting advice he receives; as a result, he will be held in little esteem.

I should like to cite a modern example of this. Father Luca,[a] adviser of the present Emperor Maximilian, speaking about His Majesty, said that he never consulted anyone, and yet never acted as he really wanted; this resulted from his failing to behave in the way I have advised above. For the Emperor is a secretive man; he does not let anyone know what plans he has, and he does not seek advice. However, as he begins to carry out his plans, those in his court get to know about them, and then advise him to act differently. And since he is not of firm character, he allows himself to be dissuaded. This is why what he orders one day is countermanded the next, why it is never known what he wants or proposes to do, and why nobody can rely upon his decisions.

A ruler, then, should never lack advice, but should have it when he wants it, not when others want to give it; rather, he should discourage anyone from giving advice uninvited. Nevertheless, he should be very ready to seek information and opinions and to listen patiently to candid views about matters that he raises. Indeed, if he learns that anyone is reticent for any reason, he should be angry.

Although many hold that a ruler may properly be considered shrewd because of the high quality of his advisers, and not because he himself is shrewd, this is undoubtedly a mistaken view. For it is an infallible rule that a prince who is not himself wise cannot be soundly advised, unless he happens to put himself in the hands of a man who is very able and controls everything. Then he could certainly be well advised, but he would not last long, because such a governor would soon deprive him of his state. But if a ruler who is not shrewd takes advice from several men, he will always hear conflicting opinions, and will be incapable of reconciling them. For his advisers will all be thinking primarily of their own interests; and he will not understand this tendency or be able to control them. And this is inevitable because men will always prove of doubtful loyalty unless compelled to be faithful. Therefore, it should be concluded that good advice, from whomsoever it may come, must have its source in the shrewdness of the ruler; the ruler's shrewdness cannot derive from sound advice.

[a *Pre' Luca*: Luca Rinaldi. (*Pre'* = *prete*, 'priest'.)]

CHAPTER XXIV

Why the rulers of Italy have lost their states

If the above-mentioned measures[a] are put into practice skilfully, they will make a new ruler seem very well established, and will quickly make his power more secure and stable than if he had always been a ruler. The actions of a new ruler are much more closely observed than those of an hereditary ruler. And if his actions are thought to be those of an able man, people are much more impressed and much more attached to him than if he had been of ancient lineage. For men are much more interested in present things than in those that are past, and if they find that their affairs are flourishing, they are content and do not seek changes. Indeed, they will do everything possible to defend a new ruler, as long as he is not deficient in other respects. Thus he will acquire a double glory: both for having founded a new principality, and for having adorned and strengthened it with good laws, strong arms, reliable allies and exemplary conduct. But a man who inherits a principality and loses it through lack of foresight and skill incurs a double disgrace.

If one considers those Italian rulers who have lost power in recent times, such as the King of Naples,[b] the Duke of Milan[c] and others, one finds in them, first, a common military weakness, for the reasons that have been discussed at length;[d] secondly, one finds that some of them had the people hostile to them, and that others, although they kept the people friendly, were unable to secure their position against the nobles. For without these weaknesses, states that have the capacity to maintain an army in the field are not lost. Philip of Macedon (not the father of Alexander, but the one defeated by Titus Quintus)[e] did not have much power and territory, compared with the might of Rome and Greece, which attacked him. Nevertheless, because he was a genuine warrior, and knew how to win over the people and how to deal with the nobles,

---

[a M. refers to all the preceding chapters, but perhaps esp. to Chs. XXI–XXIII.]
[b Frederick I of Aragon.]
[c Ludovico Sforza, called il Moro.]   [d In Chs. XIII and XIV.]
[e Philip V, King of Macedon; defeated in the battle of Cynoscephalae, in 197 B.C. See also *Disc.* II, 1; III, 10.]

he was able to carry on the war against them for many years. And although he eventually lost control of some cities, he still kept his Kingdom.

Therefore, those of our rulers who lost their principalities, after having ruled them for many years, should not lament their bad luck but should blame their own indolence.*[a]* For in quiet times they never thought that things could change (it is a common human failing when the weather is fine not to reckon on storms). When difficult times came, they thought only of fleeing and not of defending themselves; and they hoped that the people, angered by the arrogant conduct of the conquerors, would restore them to power.*[b]* This policy is sound if no other is possible, but it is very bad to neglect other policies and choose this one. A man should never risk falling because he thinks it likely that he will be rescued. This may not happen, but even if it does it will not make you secure; such a defence is weak and cowardly, because it is outside your control. Only those defences that are under your control and based on your own ability are effective, certain and lasting.

CHAPTER XXV

How much power fortune has over human affairs, and how it should be resisted

I am not unaware that many have thought, and many still think, that the affairs of the world are so ruled by fortune and by God*[c]* that the ability of men cannot control them. Rather, they think that we have no remedy at all; and therefore it could be concluded that it is useless to sweat much over things, but let them be governed by fate. This opinion has been more popular in our own times because of the great changes that have taken place*[d]* and are still to be seen even now, which could hardly

---

[*[a]* *ignavia*: see M.'s sharp comments on the habits of Italian rulers at the end of Bk VII of the *Art of War*.]

[*[b]* M. refers to the rulers of Naples and Milan just mentioned, particularly to Ludovico il Moro.]

[*[c]* *e da Dio*: these words are not in the early Charlecote MS, and may have been inserted posthumously, when the book was published in 1532; as J. H. Whitfield (*Discourses on Machiavelli*, p. 222) notes, there are no other references to God in this chapter.]

[*[d]* I.e., since 1494, when the invasions of Italy began.]

have been predicted. When I think about this, I am sometimes inclined, to some extent, to share this opinion. Nevertheless, so as not to eliminate human freedom, I am disposed to hold that fortune is the arbiter of half our actions, but that it lets us control roughly the other half.[a]

I compare fortune to one of those dangerous rivers[b] that, when they become enraged, flood the plains, destroy trees and buildings, move earth from one place and deposit it in another. Everyone flees before it, everyone gives way to its thrust, without being able to halt it in any way. But this does not mean that, when the river is not in flood, men are unable to take precautions, by means of dykes and dams, so that when it rises next time, it will either not overflow its banks or, if it does, its force will not be so uncontrolled or damaging.

The same happens with fortune, which shows its powers where no force has been organised to resist it, and therefore strikes in the places where it knows that no dykes or dams have been built to restrain it. And if you consider Italy, which has been the seat of these changes, and which has given rise to them,[c] you will see a countryside devoid of any embankments or defences. If it had been protected by proper defences, like Germany, Spain and France, the flood would not have caused such great changes or it would not have occurred at all. But I have said enough in general terms about resisting fortune.

Considering the matter in more detail, I would observe that one sees a ruler flourishing today and ruined tomorrow, without his having changed at all in character or qualities. I believe this is attributable, first, to the cause previously discussed at length,[d] namely, that a ruler who trusts entirely to luck comes to grief when his luck runs out. Moreover, I believe that we are successful when our ways are suited to the times and circumstances, and unsuccessful when they are not. For one sees that, in the things that lead to the end which everyone aims at, that is, glory and riches, men proceed in different ways: one man cautiously, another impetuously; one man forcefully, another cunningly; one man patiently, another impatiently, and each of these

[a The power of *fortuna* varies according to how much *virtú* there is in a country. Germany, Spain and France were well equipped in this respect, whereas Italy was not.]
[b I.e., mountain torrents.]
[c M. alludes to the ambitious conduct of Ludovico il Moro (who encouraged the intervention of Charles VIII; see also *Ist. fior.* VIII, 36), and later that of Alexander VI and Julius II.]
[d See p. 84.]

different ways of acting can be effective. On the other hand, of two cautious men, one may achieve his aims and the other fail. Again, two men may both succeed, although they have different characters, one acting cautiously and the other impetuously. The reason for these different outcomes is whether their ways of acting conform with the conditions in which they operate. Consequently, as I have said, two men, acting differently, may achieve the same results; and if two men act in the same way, one may succeed and the other fail. From this, again, arise changes in prosperity; because if a man acts cautiously and patiently, and the times and circumstances change in ways for which his methods are appropriate, he will be successful. But if the times and circumstances change again, he will come to grief, because he does not change his methods. And one does not find men who are so prudent that they are capable of being sufficiently flexible: either because our natural inclinations are too strong to permit us to change, or because, having always fared well by acting in a certain way, we do not think it a good idea to change our methods. Therefore, if it is necessary for a cautious man to act expeditiously, he does not know how to do it; this leads to his failure. But if it were possible to change one's character to suit the times and circumstances, one would always be successful.

Pope Julius II always acted impetuously, and found the times and circumstances so suited to his ways that he was always successful. Consider the first expedition he made to Bologna,[a] while messer Giovanni Bentivoglio was still alive. The Venetians were opposed to it, and so was the King of Spain; there were also discussions with the King of France about such an enterprise. Nevertheless, acting with his usual indomitable spirit and impetuosity, he led the expedition personally. This initiative caught the King of Spain and the Venetians off guard and constrained them to be passive spectators, the latter through fear and the former because of his desire to recover the whole of the Kingdom of Naples. On the other hand, Julius involved the King of France: for that King saw the Pope moving and, because he wanted to cultivate the Pope's friendship with a view to reducing the power of Venice, he decided that he could not refuse him troops without offending him very openly. With this swift initiative, then, Julius achieved what no other pope, acting with consummate prudence, could have attained. If he had not left Rome until everything had been agreed and

[a In 1506. See also *Disc.* I, 27.]

settled, as any other pope would have done, he would never have succeeded. For the King of France would have contrived to find countless excuses, and the others would have produced countless reasons why the Pope should hesitate. I shall not discuss his other actions, which were similar in character, and all turned out well for him. The shortness of his pontificate*ᵃ* did not permit him to taste of failure. But if circumstances had changed so that it was imperative to act cautiously, he would have been undone; for he would never have deviated from the methods that were natural to him.

I conclude, then, that since circumstances vary and men when acting lack flexibility, they are successful if their methods match the circumstances and unsuccessful if they do not. I certainly think that it is better to be impetuous*ᵇ* than cautious, because fortune is a woman, and if you want to control her, it is necessary to treat her roughly. And it is clear that she is more inclined to yield to men who are impetuous than to those who are calculating. Since fortune is a woman, she is always well disposed towards young men,*ᶜ* because they are less cautious and more aggressive, and treat her more boldly.

CHAPTER XXVI

Exhortation to liberate Italy from the barbarian yoke

Bearing in mind all the matters previously discussed, I ask myself whether the present time is appropriate for welcoming a new ruler in Italy, and whether there is matter that provides an opportunity for a far-seeing and able man to mould it into a form that will bring honour to him and benefit all its inhabitants. It seems to me that so many things are propitious for a new ruler that I am not aware that there has ever been a more appropriate time than this.

I have maintained*ᵈ* that the Israelites had to be enslaved in Egypt

[*ᵃ* *vita*: lit., 'life'. See also p. 41.]   [*ᵇ* As Julius was.]
[*ᶜ* The idea that *fortuna* is a friend of young men is also expressed in M.'s play *Clizia*, IV, 1.]
[*ᵈ* See p. 20.]

87

before the ability of Moses could be displayed, the Persians had to be oppressed by the Medes before Cyrus's greatness of spirit could be revealed, and the Athenians in disarray before the magnificent qualities of Theseus could be demonstrated. Likewise, in order for the valour and worth of an Italian spirit to be recognised, Italy had to be reduced to the desperate straits in which it now finds itself: more enslaved than the Hebrews, more oppressed than the Persians, more scattered than the Athenians, without an acknowledged leader, and without order or stability, beaten, despoiled, lacerated, overrun, in short, utterly devastated. And although recently a spark was revealed in one man that might have led one to think that he was ordained by God to achieve her redemption, yet it was seen that he was struck down by misfortune at the highest point of his career.[a] Thus, remaining almost lifeless, Italy is waiting for someone to heal her wounds, and put an end to the ravaging of Lombardy, to the extortions in the Kingdom of Naples and Tuscany, and to cure the sores that have been festering for so long. Look how Italy beseeches God to send someone to rescue her from the cruel and arrogant domination of the foreigners. Again, see how ready and willing she is to rally to a standard, if only there is someone to lead the way.

There is no one in whom Italy can now place any hope except your illustrious family which (because it is successful and talented, and favoured by God and by the Church, of which it is now head)[b] can take the lead in saving her. It will not be very difficult, if you bear in mind the deeds and lives of the men named above.[c] Although they were exceptional and remarkable men, they were still only human, and all of them had less favourable opportunities than the one that now exists, for their causes were not more righteous than this one, nor easier, nor more favoured by God. This is a very righteous cause: 'iustum enim est bellum quibus necessarium, et pia arma ubi nulla nisi in armis spes est'.[d] Circumstances are now very favourable indeed, and the difficulties to be confronted cannot be very great when the circumstances are propitious, if only your family will imitate the methods of the men I have proposed as exemplars. Moreover, very unusual events, which are signs

[a Probably a reference to Cesare Borgia.]
[b Giovanni de' Medici had become Pope Leo X in March 1513.]
[c Moses, Cyrus and Theseus.]
[d Livy, IX, 1: 'necessary wars are just wars, and when there is no other hope except in arms, they too become holy'.]

from God, have recently been observed here: the sea has opened; a cloud has shown you the way; water has flowed from the rock; manna has rained down here.[a] Everything points to your future greatness. But you must play your part, for God does not want to do everything, in order not to deprive us of our freedom and the glory that belong to us.

It is not very surprising that none of the Italians previously mentioned[b] was able to achieve what it is hoped your illustrious family will achieve, or that in all the great changes that have occurred in Italy and all the military campaigns, it always seems as if Italian military skill and valour no longer exist.

The reason for this is that our old military practices were unsound, and there has been nobody capable of devising new ones. Nothing brings so much honour to a new ruler as new laws and new practices that he has devised. Such things, if they are solidly based and conduce to achieving greatness, will make him revered and admired; and in Italy there is no lack of matter to shape into any form.

Here individuals have great skill and valour; it is the leaders who lack these qualities. Look how in duels and combats between several men[c] Italians are superior in strength, skill and resourcefulness. But when it comes to fighting in armies, they do not distinguish themselves. And all this stems from the weakness of the leaders: those who are capable are not followed, and everyone thinks that he knows best. Until now nobody has had sufficient ability or luck to succeed in imposing himself to such an extent that the other leaders have recognised his superiority. The outcome has been that, for a long time, in all the wars that have been fought during the last twenty years, any armies composed only of Italian troops have always fared badly. What happened on the Taro, and at Alessandria, Capua, Genoa, Vailà, Bologna and Mestre[d] all confirm this judgement.

If your illustrious family, then, wants to emulate those great men[e]

[a] All these images recall the journey of the Israelites from Egypt to the Promised Land.]
[b] E.g., Francesco Sforza and Cesare Borgia (see p. 23).]
[c] M. probably had esp. in mind the famous combat in 1503, at Barletta in Apulia, in which thirteen Italian knights defeated thirteen Frenchmen.]
[d] M. alludes to the battle of Fornovo, on the river Taro (1495), where Charles VIII's army succeeded in escaping, and returned to France; Alessandria was conquered by the French in 1499; Capua was sacked by the French in 1501; Genoa surrendered to the French in 1507; Bologna was taken by the French in 1511; Mestre was destroyed by the Spaniards in 1513.]
[e] Moses, Theseus and Cyrus.]

who saved their countries, it is essential above all else, as a sound basis for every campaign, to form an army composed of your own men,[a] for there can be no soldiers more loyal, more reliable or better. Even if each of these soldiers individually is brave, they will combine to form a better fighting force if they are led by their own ruler, and honoured and well treated by him. Hence, if Italian skill and courage is to protect us from foreign enemies, it is essential to form an army of this kind.

Although the Swiss and Spanish infantry are considered very formidable, both have weaknesses, so a different kind of army could not only fight them, but be confident of defeating them. For the Spaniards are very vulnerable against cavalry, and the Swiss lack confidence against infantry that fight as strongly as they do themselves. Thus, it has been seen, and experience will confirm it, that the Spaniards are very vulnerable against the French cavalry, and the Swiss have a fatal weakness against the Spanish infantry. And although there is no proof of the latter weakness, some evidence is provided by the battle of Ravenna,[b] when the Spanish infantry fought against the German battalions, which fight in the same way as the Swiss. In this battle, the Spaniards, using their agility and helped by their use of bucklers,[c] penetrated under the long German pikes, and were able to inflict great damage. The Germans were unable to repel them, and if the cavalry had not attacked the Spaniards, the Germans would all have been killed. Once the weaknesses of both the Spanish and the Swiss infantry are recognised, then, it will be possible to form a new kind of infantry, which should be able to resist cavalry charges and not be intimidated by infantry. It will be possible to do this by the right choice of weapons and by changing battle formations. It is the introduction of such new methods of fighting that enhances the reputation of a new ruler, establishing him as a great leader.

This opportunity to provide Italy with a liberator, then, after such a long time, must not be missed. I have no doubt at all that he would be received with great affection in all those regions that have been inundated by the foreign invasions, as well as with a great thirst for revenge, with resolute fidelity, with devotion and with tears of gratitude. What gate would be closed to him? What people would fail to obey him? What envious hostility would work against him? What Italian would deny him

---

[a See Ch. XIII.]   [b 11 April 1512.]
[c 'Small round shields usually held by a handle' (C.O.D.).]

homage? This foreign domination stinks in the nostrils of everyone. Let your illustrious family, then, take up this mission, with the spirit and courage and the faith that inspires all just causes, so that under your standard our country may be ennobled, and under your auspices these words of Petrarch will come true:

> Virtú contro a furore
> prenderà l'arme; e fia el combatter corto:
> ché l'antico valore
> nelli italici cor non è ancor morto.[a]

[a Petrarch, *Italia mia (Ai Signori d'Italia)*, verses 93–6: 'Valour will take up arms against wild attacks; and the battle will be short: for the ancient valour is still strong in Italian hearts.']

APPENDIX A

Letters relevant to *The Prince*

1 Niccolò Machiavelli to Francesco Vettori, then Florentine envoy to the Holy See, 10 December 1513

This letter was written in response to a letter by Vettori, dated 23 November, in which Vettori described his life in Rome. Machiavelli describes how he spends his mornings on his property, supervising work, and reading poets such as Dante, Petrarch, Tibullus and Ovid, and his afternoons in the nearby tavern, drinking and playing cards; then he turns to his work in the evenings.

When evening comes, I return home and enter my study; before I go in I remove my everyday clothes, which are very muddy and soiled, and put on clothes that are fit for a royal court. Being thus properly clad, I enter the ancient courts of the men of old, in which I am received affectionately by them and partake of the food that properly belongs to me, and for which I was born. There I do not hesitate to converse with them, and ask them why they acted as they did; and out of kindness they respond. For four hours I experience no boredom, I forget all my troubles and my fear of poverty, and death holds no more terrors for me: I am completely absorbed in them.

Since Dante[a] says that there can be no real knowledge if what has been learned is not retained, I have written down what has been valuable in their conversations, and have composed a little book *On Principalities*,[b] in which I delve as deeply as I can into this subject, and discuss what a principality is, how many different types there are, how they are gained, how they are held,

[a] Dante, *Paradiso*, V, 41–2; 'ché non fa scienza, sanza lo ritenere, avere inteso.']
[b] *De principatibus.*]

and why they are lost. And if any of my pieces*ᵃ* have ever pleased you, this one should be to your taste. Moreover, it should be welcome to a ruler, especially to a new one. Accordingly, I am dedicating it to His Magnificence Giuliano.*ᵇ* Filippo Casavecchia has seen it; he could tell you something about the work itself, and the discussions I have had with him about it, even though I am still revising and adding to it.

Honoured Ambassador, you want me to abandon this life and come to enjoy life with you. I shall certainly do so, but at present I am engaged with certain matters; however, in about six weeks they should be resolved. What makes me hesitate is that the Soderini are there,*ᶜ* and if I went there I should be obliged to visit them and speak with them. I am afraid that on my return I would not dismount at home but at the Bargiello.*ᵈ* For although this regime is very solidly based and is very stable, it is still new and therefore suspicious. Moreover, there are plenty of know-alls (like Pagolo Bertini) who, so as to be thought clever, would act in a way that might get me into trouble.*ᵉ* I hope that you will be able to allay these fears; if so, I shall certainly come to see you during the period I have indicated.

I have discussed this little work of mine with Filippo,*ᶠ* and also whether it is a good idea to present it or not;*ᵍ* and if so, whether I should take it personally or send it instead. One reason for not presenting it is my fear that Giuliano might not read it, and then that Ardinghelli*ʰ* might appropriate for himself any credit arising from this latest labour of mine. An argument for presenting it is that I am pressed by need, for I find myself in difficulties, and if my present condition persists for very long my poverty will make me despised;*ⁱ* there is also my desire that these Medici rulers should begin to use me, even if they should start by making me roll a stone.*ʲ* If I did not then win them over, I should have only myself to blame. This work, if they should read it, will reveal that I have not been asleep or wasted my time

[*ᵃ* *ghiribizzo*: this word implies a work that is not very serious, but perhaps it is merely a self-deprecating way of referring to his work. Cf. *opuscolo*, 'little book' (above), though this should probably be interpreted as referring to its length. Nevertheless, he twice calls it a 'treatise' (*trattato*) in the *Discourses* (II, 1; III, 42).]

[*ᵇ* Giuliano de' Medici, who died on 17 March 1516. It was probably after this date that M. dedicated the book to Lorenzo de' Medici.]

[*ᶜ* Piero Soderini, ex-*gonfaloniere* of the Florentine republic, with whom M. had been closely associated, had been living in Rome since early in 1513; his brother, Francesco, bishop of Volterra, a cardinal since 1503, also lived in Rome.]

[*ᵈ* The Palace of Justice in Florence; in short, be imprisoned.]

[*ᵉ* Pagolo Bertini was doubtless living in Rome. He was probably simply an indiscreet person, though he may have been a Medici zealot or spy. This sentence is very obscure.]

[*ᶠ* Filippo Casavecchia.]

[*ᵍ* To Giuliano de' Medici.]   [*ʰ* Pietro Ardinghelli.]

[*ⁱ* See M.'s remarks on poverty and contempt on pp. 56–7.]

[*ʲ* I.e., giving him unimportant tasks. This may be an allusion to the ceaseless toil mentioned in Dante's *Inferno*, VII, 27.]

during the fifteen years that I have been engaged in studying statecraft. And anyone should very much want to be served by a man who is very knowledgeable through profiting from the experiences of others. Moreover, no doubts should be cast on my trustworthiness because, since I have always been trustworthy, I could not now be prepared to become untrustworthy. For anyone who has been trustworthy and disinterested for forty-three years,[a] as I have, cannot change his character. And my very poverty testifies to my fidelity and disinterestedness. I should be glad, then, if you would write to me, giving your views on this subject.[b] I commend myself to you. May you flourish.

10 December 1513
Niccolò Machiavelli in Florence

2 Francesco Vettori:
letter to Niccolò Machiavelli, 18 January 1514

> In this letter, Vettori describes at length various amatory adventures. Towards the end, he mentions Machiavelli's book.

I have seen the chapters of your work, and I like it very much; but until I have the rest,[c] I do not wish to express a definite judgement.[d]

3 Niccolò Machiavelli to Giovan Battista Soderini,
c. 15 September 1506

> This important letter was long thought to have been written to Piero Soderini about November or December 1512, soon after his fall from power. However, recent research has established that it was addressed to Giovan Battista Soderini, Piero's nephew (who was then

---

[a In fact, he was then forty-four.]
[b Whether to present his book to Giuliano de' Medici.]
[c This may imply that M.'s revision of the book had not been finished, and that he had sent Vettori only the revised chapters. However, Federico Chabod, *Scritti su Machiavelli* (Turin, 1964), p. 144, suggests that M. may not have finished *transcribing* the work, for a copy would have been needed for presenting to Giuliano de' Medici.]
[d *judicio resoluto*: this may refer to the quality of the completed work or (this is more likely) to whether it would be appropriate to present it to Giuliano.]

eighteen), and that it was written in September 1506, in reply to a short letter (dated 12 September 1506) from him. Some passages, especially at the beginning, are very obscure; but it is evident that Machiavelli had been giving much thought, a good seven years before he composed *The Prince*, to several themes that were to be conspicuous in that work. It is probable that Machiavelli intended the letter to come to the attention of Piero; thus, it is unlikely that a man of thirty-seven would have been as eager as he claims to find out the opinions of such a young man on the reasons for human success and failure. The passages in square brackets were added by Machiavelli in the margins of the letter.

I have translated the text in Franco Gaeta's edition of Machiavelli's *Lettere* (Milan: Feltrinelli, 1961), pp. 228–31, but I have taken account of Gaeta's later edition of the *Lettere* (Turin: U.T.E.T., 1984), pp. 239–45, and occasionally followed it.

A letter of yours has reached me in a disguised form; but after reading ten words I knew it to be yours. I definitely think that at Piombino there are many people who will know you, and I am well aware of the impediments that you and Filippo[a] have, for I know that one of you is handicapped by the lack of light, and the other by having too much.[b] Not returning[c] until January does not upset me, provided I can start in February.[d] I am very sorry to learn about Filippo's fears,[e] and I am eagerly awaiting the outcome. Your letter was short but since I read it several times it seemed long.

[My lack of expertise makes it hard for me to interpret it.][f] It was very welcome because it has spurred me to do what I have delayed doing,[g] as you have reminded me. I realise that you have written disinterestedly. I would have been surprised at this if fate had not revealed so many different things to me. Consequently, nothing now surprises me very much, and I must

[a Filippo di Banco, a friend of Giovan Battista Soderini; they were planning a journey to Piombino.]
[b Soderini had said that one of them was holding the star and the other the sun, apparently a reference to astrological considerations about their journey. M. refers to this, but changes the sense, implying that one of them is not shrewd enough whereas the other is too shrewd.]
[c Not returning to Florence; M. was writing from Perugia.]
[d Apparently a reference to the duties M. would undertake with regard to organising a citizen militia.]
[e Filippo di Banco was involved in some legal case.]
[f Loosely, 'Anyone who cannot fence performs badly in a bout.' In Gaeta's 1961 edition, this sentence was inserted after the previous sentence (where it does not seem to make any sense). In his 1984 edition, it is indicated as belonging here, and I have put what I take M. to have meant.]
[g I.e., to write to Giovan Battista.]

confess to having enjoyed reading about and observing men's actions and their different methods.

I know you well and what compass guides your passage through life; and if it is criticised, which it should not be, I at any rate shall not criticise it, seeing to what ports it has led you, and what hopes can be entertained of you. Hence, I am looking at your conduct not from your own point of view (which sees it only as being prudent) but as it would be seen by the masses, who have to judge by results, not by the means employed.[a] [Everyone acts according to his own ideas.] Various courses of action may have the same outcome, there are different paths leading to the same place, and many men who operate differently achieve the same results; and if this view of things seemed doubtful, the actions of this Pope and their consequences have confirmed it.[b] [Do not advise anyone, or take advice from anyone, except in very general terms; everyone should act as his spirit moves him and audaciously.] Both Hannibal and Scipio were equally skilful at maintaining military discipline.[c] However, the former kept his armies united in Italy through acting cruelly, treacherously and with a complete disregard of religious principles, and was regarded with awe by various peoples, who rebelled against the Romans and rallied to him. Scipio, who acted in Spain with humanity and trustworthiness, and followed the principles of religion, was regarded in the same way by the peoples there. And both of them won countless victories. But because it is not the practice to regard the Romans as authorities, Lorenzo de' Medici[d] thought it well to disarm the people in order to hold Florence, whereas messer Giovanni Bentivoglio armed the people in order to hold Bologna. Vitelli[e] in Città di Castello, and the present Duke of Urbino,[f] destroyed the fortresses in their territories in order to keep power, whereas Count Francesco[g] in Milan, and many others, have built them in their territories in order to protect themselves. [Take risks,[h] because fortune is well disposed towards young men, and adapt to the times. But one cannot both have fortresses and not have them, nor be both cruel and merciful.] The Emperor Titus[i] thought he would lose power if a day passed without his having benefited someone; others have thought that benefiting anyone would undermine their power. Many

[a See p. 63.]
[b M. alludes to the expedition of Julius II to Perugia to remove its ruler, Gianpaolo Baglioni. He was then accompanying the papal forces.]
[c However, in Ch. XVII of *The Prince*, M. emphasises that Scipio was bad at maintaining military discipline.]
[d Lorenzo the Magnificent.] [e Niccolò Vitelli. See p. 75.]
[f Guido Ubaldo da Montefeltro. See p. 75.]
[g Francesco Sforza, who had been Count of Poppi. See p. 75.]
[h *tentare la fortuna*: in this sentence *fortuna* is used in two senses. See pp. 87, 104–6.]
[i Titus Flavius Sabinus Vespasianus.]

men achieve their ends by acting very cautiously. [As their luck runs out, men, families, cities come to grief. The success of everybody depends on how they act, and everyone runs out of luck; when this happens one must try to succeed by resorting to other methods. Comparison of the horse and bit with fortresses.[a]]

The present Pope, who has neither a pair of scales nor a yardstick in his house,[b] and lacks his own forces, through sheer good luck achieves what it is very difficult to achieve even with effective military forces and by acting in an orderly way.

All the above-mentioned men, and countless others who could be cited, have acquired kingdoms or territories (and still do so), and sometimes fail when unexpected events occur. Sometimes when they have succeeded their methods have been praised, and when they failed the same methods were criticised severely. And sometimes when they failed, after flourishing for a long time, no criticism at all was levelled at them, and it was said to be the will of Heaven and a consequence of fate. I do not know why it should happen that different ways of acting are sometimes both successful and sometimes both unsuccessful,[c] but I would certainly like to know. I shall be so bold as to offer you my opinions on this matter so that I can learn what you think.

I believe that just as nature makes men with different faces, it also produces different kinds of mind and temperament. Consequently, every man acts in accordance with the bent of his mind and temperament. Thus, since the times and conditions vary, some men achieve their aims completely, if their ways of acting are appropriate for the times. On the other hand, a man whose ways of acting are ill-suited to the times and circumstances will be unsuccessful. Hence, it may very well happen that two men who act in different ways will achieve the same results, for each of these ways may be appropriate for the conditions in which he finds himself, given that conditions differ as widely as countries or states do. But because the times and conditions often change (both generally and in particular places), and men do not change either their ideas or their methods, it happens that a man sometimes succeeds and at other times fails. Indeed, anyone who was shrewd enough to understand the times and circumstances, and was capable of adapting to them, would always be successful (or, at least, he would be able to avoid failure), and it would then be true that a wise man could control the stars and fates. But such shrewd men are not to be found: first, because men are short-sighted, and secondly because they cannot

[a See p. 75.]
[b I.e., who does not weigh up situations carefully, who is impetuous.]
[c This theme is developed at length in Ch. XXV.]

change their own characters. It follows that fortune[a] is changeable and dominates men, keeping them under its yoke. I think the above examples suffice to confirm this view. I have based my views on them, and I think the examples support the conclusion.

Cruel, treacherous and irreligious deeds increase the prestige of a new master of a country in which humanity, trustworthiness and religion have long ceased to have any force. On the other hand, conduct that is in accordance with humanity, trustworthiness and religion is damaging to one's prestige in a country in which cruelty, treachery and irreligion have been dominant for a long time. For just as bitter things taste disagreeable and sweet things cloy, so too men become bored in good times yet complain about hard times. These causes (as well as others) opened up Italy to Hannibal and Spain to Scipio; and the methods of both of them were suited to the time and their situations. In those times, a Scipio would not have prospered in Italy as well as Hannibal did, and a man like Hannibal would not have fared so well in Spain as Scipio did.

[a] Up to this point, M. has been using *fortuna* mostly in the sense of 'success' or 'failure'. Here it means both (i) an external force that, to a great extent, controls human affairs and (ii) the changing circumstances themselves. It may be observed, first, that it would have needed a more philosophically sophisticated mind than M. possessed to avoid such a confusion; secondly, that the various senses in which *fortuna* was then used increased the likelihood of confusion. See pp. 104–6.]

APPENDIX B

Notes on the vocabulary of *The Prince*

The purpose of this appendix is to help readers who have little or no Italian, but wish to penetrate below the surface of the translated text, to gain some understanding of most of the key-terms used in *The Prince*, particularly those that have several senses, and those that (unlike *gloria* and *reputazione*) have no exact English equivalents or else have equivalents that it is often or usually inappropriate to use. Examples of the last category are *virtú* (which can very rarely be rendered by 'virtue') and *fortuna* (for which I have only occasionally used 'fortune'). These terms, and the ideas that they denote, have been much discussed by Machiavelli scholars, but anyone who is obliged to rely on an unannotated translation cannot fail to have an imperfect grasp of their place in *The Prince*. These notes, then, give some indications of the ways in which I have translated most of the more important terms in *The Prince*, and are designed to enable the more curious reader to grasp better the complexities and ambiguities of these terms, and the ideas that they denote.

principe, signore

Principe usually denotes a 'ruler'. In *The Prince*, it almost always denotes a ruler of a monarchical type, one who rules a 'principality' (*principato*), 'kingdom' (*regno*), 'monarchy' (*monarchia*) or 'empire' (*imperio*); I have almost always rendered it as 'ruler', though in a few places I have used 'prince' (e.g., pp. 5, 18). (In the *Discourses*, it also sometimes denotes rulers of republics.)[a]

But *principe* is also used to denote a 'head' or 'leader' of any kind: thus the generals Philopoemen (p. 53) and Hannibal (p. 60) are each called *principe*.

[a E.g., I, 12; II, 2.]

The wide reference of this word derives from the usage of the Latin word *princeps*.

Signore is frequently used in *The Prince*. Unlike *principe*, it always denotes a ruler of a monarchical type. When it is used as an exact synonym of *principe*, I have usually rendered it as 'ruler'. Sometimes it is used to denote a petty ruler or feudal lord: in these cases I have translated it as 'lord' (pp. 26, 40) or 'noble' (p. 16). *Signore* also denotes a ruler of a conquered or annexed territory, and here I have usually rendered it as 'master' (pp. 12–15, 27).

principato

Principato usually denotes a state of a monarchical type (whether large or small, old or new, unitary or mixed) that is ruled by a *principe*, 'king' (*re*) or 'emperor' (*imperatore*). It is usually rendered in English as 'principality', and this is how I have translated it, though with some misgivings, for this term is usually used today with regard to very small hereditary monarchical states (e.g., Monaco, Lichtenstein); but the alternative, 'principate' (because of its association with the early Roman Empire), would be perhaps even more misleading.

Secondly, *principato* is sometimes used to denote power in such a 'principality', or the office of *principe*. (Instances of this sense are found mostly in Chapters VIII, IX and XIX.) Thus, Machiavelli discusses in Chapter IX the position of a man who *viene al principato* through the help of the nobles and that of a man who *arriva al principato* with popular support: I have translated these phrases as 'becomes ruler' (p. 35). Again, in Chapter XIX, Machiavelli refers to those who *venivano al principato* 'as new men': I have rendered this phrase as 'came to the throne' (p. 67).

imperio

Imperio, which derives from the Latin *imperium*, has two main senses. First, it denotes 'power', 'rule' or 'dominion' exercised by a ruler (or rulers) over the inhabitants of his (or their) own state, that is, over subjects or citizens. Thus, in Chapter VII, Machiavelli speaks of those who *sono ascesi allo imperio* 'through favour or luck and through the arms of others': this phrase means 'have risen to power' or 'have become rulers'. Again, he says in Chapter VIII that, by acting as Agathocles did, one may gain *imperio*, but not glory; I have rendered this as 'power' (p. 31). This sense of *imperio* is very similar to the second sense of *principato* that I have distinguished (see above), and I have usually translated it as 'power'. Although this sense of *imperio* normally denotes primarily 'political power' (it also implies having military forces at one's disposal, of course), there is a passage in Chapter XVII in which the word is used with reference to Scipio's 'military command' (see p. 60).

Secondly, *imperio* denotes 'power', 'rule' or 'dominion' exercised by one state over another or several states. Thus, Machiavelli observes in Chapter XII that, using mercenaries, the Venetians and Florentines had *cresciuto l'imperio loro*, that is, subjugated or annexed neighbouring states: I have translated this phrase as 'augmented their dominions' (p. 45). There is another use of *imperio* that seems best classified with this second sense: Machiavelli sometimes uses *imperio* to denote 'empire'. (*Impero* was an exceedingly rare word before the sixteenth century, and its present sense of 'empire', or monarchical state that rules over other states, does not seem to have become fixed before the late eighteenth century.) Thus, in Chapter XIII he observes that the practice of using the Goths as soldiers had the effect of sapping 'the strength of the Roman Empire' (*imperio romano*) (p. 51).

stato

Stato is used in *The Prince* in two main senses. It denotes a political community existing within certain territorial boundaries as well as the government of such a community. (These are also the two main political senses of the English term 'state', used since the mid-sixteenth century.)

I have usually translated the first sense as 'state', but sometimes I have used 'territory' and 'region'. But the second sense is rather more common, and I have rendered it by 'government' and 'power', and occasionally by 'office' (p. 40) and 'regime' (p. 75). *Stato* is also used to denote a type of government: e.g., *uno stato di pochi* (lit., 'a state of [a] few'), which I have rendered as 'an oligarchical government' and 'oligarchies' (p. 18).

Sometimes *stato* combines two senses: thus, I have rendered *tanto stato* as 'sufficient territory and power' (p. 38), *più stato* as 'more territory and power' (p. 40), *molto stato* as 'much power and territory' (p. 83).

Stato is also used to denote 'politics' and 'statecraft'. In his famous letter to Vettori (Dec. 1513),[a] Machiavelli says that for fifteen years he has been engaged in studying *l'arte dello stato*, i.e., 'statecraft'. In Chapter III of *The Prince*, he uses the phrase *nelle cose di stato* ('in affairs of state', p. 11), and at the end of this chapter he contrasts understanding *la guerra*, 'warfare', with understanding *lo stato*, i.e., 'politics' or 'statecraft' (p. 14).[b]

[a See p. 95.]
[b In *Disc.* III, 40, Machiavelli says that 'half measures' (*la via del mezzo*) are always harmful *nelle cose di stato*, and here the phrase also denotes 'warfare'.]

Finally, Machiavelli occasionally seems to use *stato* rather loosely. in Chapter IV, discussing the frequent rebellions against the Romans in Spain, Gaul and Greece, he says that there were many principalities in those *stati*: I have rendered this as 'countries', because they were not 'political communities' as defined above. There are three other passages in which *stato* appears to denote a geographical 'area' or 'region' rather than a 'political community': *lo stato di Asia* (see p. 17), *lo stato di Lombardia* (p. 11) and *lo stato di Romagna* (p. 28). It is perhaps arguable that the Romagna was (or had become) a genuine political community, but I have thought it better not to translate *stato* in these three phrases.

città, provincia, patria

Città denotes a small independent state, or 'city-state', consisting of an urban area and surrounding countryside, and also a city that is not self-governing or independent, but forms part of a larger political community.

Provincia denotes any area that is larger than a 'city' or 'city-state'. Machiavelli tends to use *provincia* in the Roman way (except that the Romans would never have called Italy a *provincia*, as Machiavelli does in Chapter III). Thus, *provincia* is used with reference to large regions, such as Greece (Ch. III), and to smaller regions, such as the Romagna and Tuscany: I have used 'region' in the last two cases (pp. 26, 53), but I have usually translated *provincia* as 'country'. The noun *provinciali* is used in Chapter III to denote the 'inhabitants' of a *provincia*; more often the words *populo* and *populi* ('people', 'peoples') are used.

Patria denotes one's own city, city-state or country. It has emotional overtones that *provincia* lacks, and I have sometimes rendered it as 'own country' (pp. 20, 33–4) or 'native city' (p. 32).

virtú, virtuoso

Virtú, from the Latin *virtus* (itself derived from *vir*, 'man'), is used by Machiavelli (as well as by earlier and contemporary writers) in a variety of senses. Occasionally, it signifies 'virtue' (as opposed to *vizio*, 'vice'); instances of this sense occur in Chapters XV and XVI (see pp. 55–6). The plural, *le virtú*, usually has the sense of 'good qualities' or 'virtues'.

Much more often, however, *virtú* has various senses (which are sometimes combined): 'ability', 'skill', 'energy', 'determination', 'strength', 'spiritedness', 'courage' or 'prowess'. I have translated it in different ways, according to the context: usually I have preferred to use 'ability' (since it is most comprehensive in meaning), but when *virtú* is used in a military context I have sometimes rendered it as 'prowess' or 'courage'.

The main antonyms of this set of senses of *virtú* are *ignavia* ('indolence' or 'sloth', sometimes conjoined with, or having overtones of, 'cowardice': see p. 49), *viltà* ('baseness' or 'weakness', also with overtones of 'cowardice': see p. 84), *ozio* ('indolence') and *debolezza* ('weakness'). When a ruler lacks the various qualities that *virtú* denotes, he becomes despised (see p. 64).

It will be apparent that most of the qualities that *virtú* denotes are appropriate for a man (*vir*) to have, though the 'determination' that is implicit in Machiavelli's use of this word has overtones of 'ruthlessness', which is not a characteristic of a *good* man. *Virtú*, then, in this usual sense (or set of senses) denotes qualities that may well be combined with 'villainy' (*scelleratezza*),[a] as happened with Oliverotto Euffreducci and his mentor, Vitellozzo Vitelli (see p. 33).

Virtú has several synonyms. Thus, a man who is *animoso* ('spirited' or 'courageous'), as Sixtus IV was (p. 40), to some extent or in some respects is *virtuoso*; a *valente uomo* ('able man'), as Carmagnola was (p. 46), is indistinguishable from a *uomo virtuoso*. To possess *parte eccellentissime* ('many very fine qualities'), as Antoninus did (p. 69), is the same as possessing outstanding *virtú*. The phrase *virtú di animo e di corpo* (energy or strength of mind and body: p. 30) denotes what might be called all-round *virtú*, and *grandezza di animo* denotes a very high degree of *virtú* of spirit or character ('indomitable spirit', p. 31; 'greatness of spirit', p. 88).

Although *virtú* usually denotes various human qualities, it is occasionally used about material objects: in Chapter VI, Machiavelli speaks of skilful archers who know the *virtú* ('power' or 'strength') of their bows (p. 19). And in Chapter XIV *virtú* is used metaphorically in the sense of 'efficacy': knowledge of, and skill in, military matters is 'of such *virtú*' that it enables hereditary rulers to maintain power and 'new men' to become rulers (p. 52).

fortuna

Fortuna is used by Machiavelli (and by Italian Renaissance writers generally) in several more senses than the English word 'fortune', and it is a difficult term to translate. It is possible to distinguish six senses: a non-human 'force'; luck; favour or help; condition or conditions; circumstances; success and failure. But since good 'luck' and 'favour' often go together, since 'conditions' and 'circumstances' are sometimes only different 'aspects' of the same thing, and since 'success' and 'failure' may be regarded as particular kinds of 'condition', I have preferred to make a

[a The same combination of qualities is attributed to Severus in *Disc.* I, 10. See also pp. 68–9.]

tripartite classification, the second and third categories (especially the latter) consisting of 'sets' of senses.

First, Machiavelli sometimes speaks of *fortuna* as (or as if it were) a force or agent that intervenes in human affairs: this sense is conspicuous especially in Chapter XXV, and I have rendered it as 'fortune'.

Secondly, *fortuna* denotes 'luck' (which may be 'good' or 'bad'): in other words, events or actions (especially those that are unforeseen) that affect us, either favourably or unfavourably, but which are often beyond our control; when they are inimical, it is frequently difficult to guard against them.

We may be favourably or unfavourably affected by natural forces that do not usually have such effects (and which are therefore unexpected),[a] or we may be favourably or unfavourably affected by the actions of human beings. Others may (knowingly or unwittingly) promote or thwart our plans; they may oppose or attack us, show us favour, help us militarily or in other ways. Such 'interventions' are often unexpected or unpredictable, and they may or may not continue. Enemies may be won over; friends or allies may either cease to favour us or become unable to help us.

When *fortuna* is contrasted with *virtú* (as at the end of Chapter I), it primarily signifies 'good luck' or being 'favoured' by others, and I have usually translated it as 'luck or favour' or 'favour or luck': for *fortuna* sometimes has the combined sense of 'luck and favour', sometimes it denotes 'luck', and sometimes 'favour'. (In Chapter VIII there is a passage in which *fortuna* denotes 'favour' or, at least, includes it: Agathocles's early career is said to have owed little or nothing to *fortuna*, since he rose through his own efforts, 'not through anyone's *favore*' (p. 31).) Chapter VI deals with men who became rulers through their own *virtú*, or 'ability', and by using their own forces: they owed nothing to *fortuna*, to 'favour'[b] or to 'luck', except the good opportunities (*occasioni*) that they had. Chapter VII is concerned with men who acquired political power through 'the arms of others' and *fortuna*: I have interpreted *fortuna* here as signifying primarily 'favour', with overtones of good 'luck', for the favour of others is often not to be had. Thus, Machiavelli begins this chapter by referring to 'states' that were 'conceded' to men through favour (*grazia*) or for money (and he refers to some Roman emperors who bought power by bribing the soldiers). Such rulers, he says, depend entirely on the very unreliable support of those who 'conceded' power to them. But most of Chapter VII is devoted to the career of Cesare Borgia, who gained power through the *fortuna* of his father, Pope Alexander VI, and was ruined when this ceased, at Alexander's death, before Cesare had firmly established his power throughout his new terri-

[a See p. 108.]   [b Except Moses, who was favoured by God (see p. 20).]

tories. Here *fortuna* combines two senses: the 'powerful position' of Alexander, and the 'favour' shown Cesare by his father, who was determined to help his son set himself up as a ruler. Machiavelli attributes Cesare's downfall partly to the grave misfortune of his being incapacitated by a very serious illness (which he had no reason to expect) just when his father was dying, and partly to his culpable failure to block the election of Julius II, who was an implacable enemy of the Borgias.

'Luck' may be either 'good' or 'bad': indolent rulers who lose power may afterwards be inclined to lament their bad luck, instead of recognising their own *ignavia*, their slothful failure to use quiet times for building up their power and strengthening their defences (see pp. 54, 84). In such circumstances Machiavelli rejects the appeal to *fortuna* as providing an 'explanation' of their downfall. Rather, it is the policy of *appoggiarsi tutto in sulla fortuna* ('trusting entirely to luck': p. 85) that is a recipe for ruin.

Thirdly, there are some fairly closely related senses of *fortuna*, which it seems appropriate to classify together: 'condition' of life, a favourable or unfavourable position in relation to other men, or for attaining power; 'conditions' or 'circumstances'; and 'success' or 'failure'. Thus, as we saw, the *fortuna* of Alexander VI denotes, in part, his 'prosperity' or 'flourishing position'. Again, the 'support' of those who confer 'power' or a 'state' on others (to which I have referred) consists of *voluntà* and *fortuna*, that is, their 'goodwill' and 'prosperity'. But *fortuna* sometimes denotes a low social position, one unfavourable to becoming a ruler: a man who lives *in privata fortuna*, whose family is not involved or prominent in public life, usually has little chance of gaining power, unless he is exceptionally able, or, if he does, of keeping it (see p. 23). This was Agathocles's situation but, because his father was a potter, his *fortuna*, or 'station', was also *infima et abietta* ('of the lowest and most abject origins': p. 30). Again, *fortuna* denotes 'success' and 'failure', as in Chapter XVII: there were never any dissensions or rebellions in Hannibal's army, *cosí nella cattiva come nella sua buona fortuna* ('whether things were going well or badly' (p. 60)).

If it were possible to adapt one's character to suit 'the times and circumstances' (*li tempi e le cose*), 'one would always be successful' (*non si muterebbe fortuna*) (p. 86). Unfortunately, however, men lack the required flexibility and, 'since circumstances vary' (*variando la fortuna*), they are successful (*felici*) only when their characters and methods happen to suit the circumstances or conditions in which they operate (p. 87). The argument of Chapter XXV is coherent, I think, but the various senses in which *fortuna* is used in it need to be carefully distinguished: it denotes 'success' and 'circumstances' as well as a 'force' that (like a destructive river) intervenes in human affairs.

occasione

Occasione (from the Latin *occasio*) is a term that is closely connected with both *fortuna* and *virtú*. I have usually translated it as 'opportunity'. It is conspicuous especially in Chapter VI, in which Machiavelli discusses men who became great through their own *virtú* and by using their own forces. He says that they owed nothing to *fortuna* except the *occasione*, that is, conditions or circumstances favourable to their enterprises. Favourable conditions are necessary even for men of great ability: for 'if they had lacked the opportunity (*occasione*), the strength of their spirit (*la virtú dello animo loro*) would have been sapped (*spenta*)'. But if they had lacked such *virtú*, 'the opportunity (*occasione*) would have been wasted' (p. 20). Men of outstanding ability (*eccellente virtú*) are able to recognise opportunities and exploit them. Thus, the grave difficulties in which the Syracusans found themselves provided Hiero, a man of considerable *virtú*, with a fine opportunity to succeed as their general and then become their ruler (p. 22).

These *occasioni* may be provided by the political condition or the military situation of a country: it may be propitious for undertaking certain political initiatives or military enterprises. Or they may be specific opportunities resulting from a particular set of circumstances. 'Occasion' was often depicted as a swiftly moving woman with a forelock and no hair behind:[a] this image implies a favourable opportunity which must be recognised and seized (for it may never come again) rather than a general situation that is fairly easy to recognise (e.g., the Israelite captivity in Egypt) but requires imagination, energy and courage to change.

Cesare Borgia, a far-seeing and able man (*uno prudente e virtuoso uomo*) was very skilful at seizing favourable opportunities for eliminating enemies. Thus, 'he waited for an opportunity (*la occasione*) to destroy the leaders of the Orsini faction. . . A fine chance came, and he exploited it to the full (*la quale li venne bene, e lui l'usò meglio*)' (p. 25). Again, he availed himself of an appropriate opportunity to kill Remirro de Orco, his governor in the Romagna, who had incurred the hatred of the inhabitants and was (certainly indirectly, and perhaps also directly) undermining Cesare's power (p. 26).

necessità

There are no special difficulties involved in translating the noun *necessità*, the adjective *necessario* and the past participle *necessitato*: 'necessity' and 'necessary' are exact equivalents. It is true that 'necessitated' is not felici-

[a E.g., Marlowe, in *The Jew of Malta*, V, ii, 44–6: 'Begin betimes; Occasion's bald behind: / Slip not thine opportunity, for fear too late / Thou seek'st for much, but canst not compass it.']

tous, and I have used such words as 'obliged' and 'forced'; I have also sometimes preferred not to translate *necessità* by 'necessity' and *necessario* by 'necessary', and have used 'need' and 'constraint', and various verbal forms for the former, and 'forced', 'must' and 'essential' for the latter.

However, 'necessity' is one of the most important ideas in terms of which Machiavelli considers human conduct. And it should be emphasised that, when discussing the pressures that men operate under, he uses several other words. Thus, the verb *convenire* (especially when used – as it usually is – in the impersonal form of the third person singular, *conviene*) almost always means 'it is necessary' or 'must'. The verb *dovere*, too, sometimes signifies 'to be necessary': at times I have translated the frequently used third person singular form, *debbe*, as 'must', though more often I have interpreted it as being less 'strong', and have used 'should'. Other words that express the idea of 'necessity' are *non può, impossibile, forzato, costretto* and *bisogna*: e.g., *non ti puoi mantenere amici*, 'you cannot retain the friendship' (p. 7); *fu forzato prendere quelle amicizie che poteva*, 'he was forced to make whatever alliances he could' (p. 12); *fu costretto a seguitare*, 'he was forced to follow it up' (p. 12); *bisognando*, 'when this is necessary' (p. 38); *conviene rovini*, 'his downfall is inevitable' (pp. 54–5).

There are two kinds of 'necessity'. The first is 'absolute' or 'categorical' in character: that is, when men have no choice, when their condition is determined by natural forces (floods, earthquakes, etc.) or by powerful human forces (e.g., being defeated by a much stronger army, being expelled from one's home or native region (see p. 9)). Secondly, there is 'hypothetical' or 'conditional' necessity: some actions, policies, etc., are or become 'necessary' only if certain conditions and purposes are postulated (e.g., 'If you don't want to get wet, you must use an umbrella'). Most of the instances of 'necessity' mentioned in *The Prince* are hypothetical in character (whether or not the agents involved, or Machiavelli himself, thought of them in this way).

Thus, Louis XII was 'forced' to make whatever alliances he could because (a) he wanted to effect an entry into Italy, and (b) the conduct of his predecessor, Charles VIII, had resulted in widespread hostility towards him (see p. 12). Again, the downfall of a ruler is 'inevitable' (see p. 55) only (a) if he is surrounded by many unscrupulous men and (b) if he wants to act honourably always. And the 'need' to be prepared to act ruthlessly or immorally (mentioned in the next sentence) exists only (a) if the ruler is surrounded by rogues and (b) if he does 'want to maintain his power' (*volendosi mantenere*). If the ruler were surrounded by good men *or* if he did not want to continue to rule, there would be no 'need' for him to act in this way.

libertà, libero

The primary senses of these words are of course 'freedom' (or 'liberty') and 'free' (and they are normally used by Machiavelli with reference to communities rather than to individuals). However, they have two rather more specific senses: first, a 'republic' (as opposed to a 'principality', a 'kingdom' or 'monarchy'); secondly, a state (whether 'republic' or 'principality') that is not subject to another state, i.e., 'independent'. (*Indipendenza* and *indipendente* were not coined until near the end of the sixteenth century.)

With regard to the first sense, 'living under a *principe*' is sometimes contrasted with *vivere liberi, vivere . . . in libertà* or *essere liberi*: I have translated these phrases as 'being free' (p. 5), 'living . . . in freedom' (p. 17) and 'a free way of life' (p. 18), and also as 'governing themselves' (p. 8). In Chapter IX, Machiavelli clearly uses *libertà* to denote a 'republic' (as opposed to a 'principality', or to *licenzia*, i.e., 'anarchy', no effective government). In short, for Machiavelli, a genuine 'republic' is characterised by its 'free institutions', and by the opportunities it affords to all its citizens to participate in public life. Naturally, this theme is explored more fully in the *Discourses* (e.g. II, 2) than in *The Prince*, which is concerned almost exclusively with 'principalities'.

Frequently Machiavelli clearly uses *libertà* and *libero* to denote either 'republican freedom' or 'independence'. Sometimes they combine both senses. Thus Chapter V is concerned (as the reference to 'republics' in the last sentence confirms) with the problems confronting a ruler who has annexed a state that has been 'accustomed to living under [its] own laws and in freedom' (p. 17), in other words, an independent republic;[a] accordingly, I have translated *una città usa a vivere libera* as 'a city that is accustomed to being independent and having free institutions' (p. 18).

The adjectives *libero* and *liberissimo* are used primarily in the sense of 'independent' in Chapters X and XII. Thus, 'the cities of Germany are completely independent (*liberissime*): for they 'obey the Emperor only when they want to' (p. 38). Again, both Rome and Sparta were independent (*libere*: p. 44); but whereas Rome was a republic in which free institutions flourished, Sparta combined independence with a notorious lack of internal 'freedom'.

In addition, *libero* is used in three passages in the phrase *libero arbitrio* (literally 'free will'). In Chapter XXIII, when rulers are advised to give *libero arbitrio* to their advisers, it means 'permitting them . . . to speak frankly' (p. 81), and speaking *liberamente* (p. 81) means speaking 'candidly', without hesitation or reticence. In the other two passages, I do not think *libero*

[a Principatus, or principati, occurs in the chapter-title, but only the penultimate sentence of the chapter is concerned with principalities, and it was evidently included to emphasise the contrast with 'independent republics'.]

arbitrio possesses a narrow or technical sense: accordingly, I have translated it as 'human freedom' (p. 85) and 'our freedom' (p. 89).

licenzia, licenzioso

The main sense of *licenzia* is 'disorder' or 'anarchy' (*anarchia* was not coined until the early seventeenth century), and the word is used in this sense in Chapter IX, in which *licenzia* is contrasted with *libertà*, or a 'republic', and with a 'principality' (p. 34). Another instance of this sense, but with a more restricted reference, occurs in Chapter XVII, in which Scipio is accused of having permitted his soldiers more *licenzia* ('freedom') than is compatible with military discipline (p. 60). Again, in Chapter XIX, Machiavelli says that Commodus 'began to curry favour with the soldiers and *farli licenziosi*': that is, he 'let them behave as they liked' (p. 70). The adverb is also used to express the same idea: 'being used to doing as they pleased (*licenziosamente*) under Commodus' (p. 68), the soldiers were unwilling to accept the restrictions that Pertinax wanted to impose on them.

The adjective *licenzioso* is also used metaphorically to express the 'uncontrolled' force of a river in flood (p. 85).

ordine, ordini

The singular *ordine* usually denotes 'order': thus, Italy is now in a sorry condition, *sanza ordine* ('without order or stability': p. 88). Sometimes it denotes 'the established order' (p. 6) or 'the existing order'. Occasionally it signifies the natural *ordine* of things (p. 79) and the natural order of events ('what usually happens': p. 10).

It is the plural *ordini* that has rather more senses, and is more difficult to translate. Very frequently it signifies social and political 'institutions' or 'laws' (and the former often implies the latter). In Chapter VI, Machiavelli discusses the difficulties involved in *introdurre nuovi ordini* ('introducing a new form of government'; p. 20), and I have sometimes translated the plural form as 'order': 'the old order' (p. 21: *li vecchi ordini*) and 'the new order' (p. 21: *li ordini nuovi*). An 'order', in this sense, consists not only of a 'form of government', 'political institutions' and 'laws' but also of 'customs' and 'beliefs'. *Ordini* has all these senses in Chapter XI: ecclesiastical principalities, that is, the Papacy and its Temporal Power, are sustained by *ordini antiquati nella relligione*. I have translated this as 'ancient religious institutions' (p. 40), but here *ordini* clearly also denotes religious 'beliefs'. In one passage, *ordini* signifies ideas that have the status almost of 'rules': at the beginning of Chapter XV, Machiavelli emphasises that, in the topics he is about to discuss, he will depart from *li ordini delli altri*, that is, 'from the precepts offered by others' (p. 54). Sometimes, too, *ordini* denotes 'methods' or 'practices' (e.g., p. 51), and also 'measures' (p. 36), of various kinds.

Ordini is often used in a military context, to denote military 'institutions', 'practices' or 'formations'. After seizing power in Fermo, Oliverotto Euffreducci consolidated his position by means of new *ordini civili e militari* ('civil and military institutions': p. 33). Machiavelli discusses in Chapter XII the usual methods employed by Italian mercenaries, and remarks that 'all these practices (*cose*) were permitted *ne' loro ordini militari*' ('by the prevailing military code': p. 47). In Chapter XXVI, he maintains that Italian armies have fared badly in recent years because of the unsoundness of *li ordini antichi* of war ('our old military practices': p. 89). Machiavelli asserts in Chapter XVI that rulers should concentrate their attention on 'war and its *ordini e disciplina* ('methods and practices': p. 52). Finally, *ordine* and *ordini* sometimes denote military 'formations' or 'ways of fighting', as in the phrase *servando li ordini* ('while still preserving proper military formation': p. 53); and in Chapter XXVI Machiavelli remarks that the German battalions *servono el medesimo ordine* as the Swiss ('fight in the same way': p. 90).

spegnere

This is one of the most characteristic Machiavellian words. It always has rather sinister overtones, but its exact sense is sometimes a little unclear. *Spegnere* means 'to extinguish',[a] and Machiavelli sometimes uses it to mean 'to render powerless' (or 'to destroy' someone's power) or 'to neutralise'; but it also means 'to eliminate' or 'to kill'. Fredi Chiappelli has maintained that, for Machiavelli, *spegnere* is a technical term,[b] with the implication that it has a stable or fixed meaning. This word *may* be regarded as a technical term, in as much as a rival or enemy whom one has killed has indeed been 'neutralised' or 'rendered powerless'. Nevertheless, the *precise* sense that the word bears varies, and it is not always easy to determine (especially sometimes when the past participle *spento* is used) whether a particular person has been killed, has died naturally, or has simply been rendered powerless, and is no longer a threat. However, when *spegnere* is used with reference to groups or states, it usually has the sense of 'to neutralise' or 'to render powerless' (or 'less powerful').

In Chapters III–V, Machiavelli insists on the necessity, when annexing a

[a] It is the word normally used for 'turning off' an electric light; and the reflexive *spegnersi* denotes 'to die', being one of several alternatives to *morire*.]

[b] F. Chiappelli, *Studi sul linguaggio del Machiavelli* (Florence, 1952), pp. 56–9.]

monarchical state, of killing the ruler's family. To hold such states securely, 'it is enough to wipe out (*aver spenta*) the family of the ruler' (p. 8). Later on this page, he repeats this advice. The Orsini leaders were tricked and killed (*spenti*) by Cesare Borgia (p. 25), who also planned 'to wipe out the families (*spegnere tutti e' sangui*) of the rulers whom he had dispossessed, so that a new pope could not restore them to power' (p. 27). In fact, he 'killed (*ammazzò*) as many . . . as he was able, and very few escaped from him' (p. 27).

However, in Chapter XI, in which *spegnere* occurs five times, it means to render 'powerless' or 'impotent' (see p. 41), although of course some killing occurred in the operations described. Again, in Chapters VI, VII and XIII, *spegnere* is used to denote disbanding mercenary troops (pp. 22, 29, 49) and the French infantry (p. 50).

assicurare, assicurarsi

Machiavelli usually uses the verbs *assicurare* and *assicurarsi* (especially the latter) in senses that are now obsolete. *Assicurare* means 'to protect' or 'to defend' and also 'to assure' or 'to reassure'. Cesare Borgia, seeking to trap and kill the leaders of the Orsini faction, pretended to be reconciled with them; when he met their representative, Paulo Orsini, at Imola, he 'treated Paulo very courteously and generously, giving him money, clothes and horses, in order to reassure him' (*per assicurarlo*) (p. 25). An instance of the first sense occurs in Chapter XIX (p. 66): the reformer of the French constitution in the Middle Ages 'knew that the people hated the nobles because they were afraid of them', and 'he wanted to protect them' (*volendo assicurarli*).

The reflexive verb *assicurarsi* is used by Machiavelli in the sense of 'to protect oneself', one's life, position or power, and such 'self-protection' implies killing, eliminating or neutralising one's enemies. He says that a ruler who has reconquered a rebellious state or territory 'will be more ruthless in consolidating his power' (*meno respettivo ad assicurarsi*): 'in punishing the guilty, unmasking suspects, and remedying weaknesses in his government' (p. 7). Machiavelli says in Chapter VII that a new ruler who considers it necessary 'to deal effectively with his enemies' (*assicurarsi de' nimici*), as well as doing various other things, could not do better than imitate Cesare Borgia (p. 29). Again, in Chapter VIII (p. 33), he says that harsh or cruel deeds (*le crudeltà*) may be said to 'well committed' if they are 'all committed at once, because they are necessary for establishing one's power' (*per necessità dello assicurarsi*). And in Chapter IX Machiavelli observes that 'a ruler can never protect himself (*non si può mai assicurare*) from a hostile people, because there are too many of them; but he can protect himself (*si può assicurare*) from the nobles, because there are few of them' (p. 35). Indeed, it is essential for a ruler to know how to control and make use of the nobles, and deal effectively with those who are dangerous (see also p. 83).

Assicurarsi, then, like *spegnere*, is used by Machiavelli to denote conduct that is designed to protect oneself, although the precise character of the actions described or recommended is sometimes not specified. However, killing or neutralising rivals or enemies are very effective ways of protecting oneself.

amico, amicizia

These words usually denote 'friend' and 'friendship', and *amico* sometimes has this sense in *The Prince*. Nevertheless, at times I have translated *amico* slightly differently. Thus, I have rendered *guadagnarsi amici* as 'to win over men' (pp. 74–5), *se arà avuto el populo amico* as 'although they kept the people friendly' (p. 83) and, in Chapter XXV, where Machiavelli says that *fortuna* is always *amica de' giovani*, 'well disposed towards young men' (p. 87).

However, *amico* often signifies 'ally', and *amicizia* almost always means 'alliance'. (*Alleanza* was not coined until the seventeenth century, and *alleato* was scarcely used before the same period.)[a] When Machiavelli discusses or refers to relations between rulers, *amico* and *amicizia* should usually be taken to mean 'ally' and 'alliance', although 'friendly relations' rather than a 'formal alliance' is doubtless sometimes meant.

[a The *Grande dizionario della lingua italiana* cites a thirteenth-century instance of *alleato* in the sense of 'ally', but no other pre-seventeenth-century instances are given.]

Biographical notes[a]

These notes are intended to provide the reader with a modicum of information about the men and women discussed or mentioned in the text of *The Prince* and in the footnotes. They are primarily of a biographical character, though the course of events has not been altogether neglected. I have usually given fewer details about the men of the Ancient World, since the emphasis of the book is 'modern'. And sometimes as much space is devoted to less important as to famous persons, on whom most encyclopedias and biographical dictionaries have articles (sometimes lengthy ones). *A Concise Encyclopedia of the Italian Renaissance*, ed. J. R. Hale (London: Thames & Hudson, 1981), may profitably be consulted. A few minor figures have been omitted, because I have been unable to find reliable information or anything at all. The *Dizionario biografico degli Italiani* has reached only the letter D (after thirty-two volumes), and this has handicapped me in the preparation of these notes. I have given details about the matrimonial links between various Italian rulers, and about the frequent movements of mercenary leaders from one employer to another.

AESCULAPIUS. Legendary Greek hero, said to have been Apollo's son, and brought up by Chiron, who taught him hunting and the art of healing.

AGATHOCLES (361–289 B.C.), ruler of Syracuse. Born at Thermae Himeraeae, in Sicily. His father, who was a potter, moved to Syracuse, where Agathocles followed the same trade for a time, before entering the army. He was twice exiled for attempting to overthrow the oligarchical govern-

---

[a] I am indebted to Dr Cecil H. Clough for information about some dates of births and deaths, and to Dr Silvana Palmerio, of the Istituto della Enciclopedia Italiana, for sending me two entries from the *Dizionario biografico*.

ment, but in 317 he seized power. Eventually he controlled most of Sicily, and declared himself King of Sicily about 304. In 310 he was defeated at Himera by the Carthaginians, who then besieged Syracuse. Agathocles, however, broke through the blockade with part of his army, and went to Africa, where he won several victories against Carthage.

ALBERICO DA BARBIANO, Count of Conio (1348–1409), mercenary leader. Born at Barbiano, in the Romagna, in 1376 he fought with Sir John Hawkwood in the Romagna, in the service of the Papacy. But, disturbed by the devastation caused by foreign mercenaries, he formed a force of Italian mercenaries, which was called the Company of St. George. Within about twenty years most of the mercenary forces fighting in Italy were composed of Italians. He fought for Bernabò Visconti, Gian Galeazzo Visconti (from 1392 until 1402), the Papacy and the Kingdom of Naples.

ALEXANDER III, King of Macedon, called 'the Great' (356–323 B.C.). Son of Philip II of Macedon; for about three or four years he had Aristotle as tutor, and in 336 he succeeded his father. He crossed the Hellespont in 334, and conquered Syria, Phoenicia and Egypt, before striking at Persia itself, which he conquered in 330.

ALEXANDER VI, POPE: RODRIGO BORGIA, Span. DE BORJA (1431–1503). Born near Valencia, in Aragon, he came to Italy about 1451 or 1452, and graduated in canon law at Bologna University in 1456. In April 1455 his uncle, Cardinal Alfonso de Borja, became Pope Calixtus III. Calixtus's reputation is marred only by his nepotism. In 1456 he made his nephew a cardinal, in 1457 leader of the papal army and vice-chancellor of the Church; Borgia was considered to have been an efficient administrator. During the 1460s he fathered three children by an unknown mistress (or mistresses), and about 1473 he began a long liaison with Vannozza Catanei, who bore him four children (including Cesare and Lucrezia). After he became pope, in 1492, he was much concerned with advancing his children (for Cesare, see pp. 23–9). The evil ways of the papal court were strongly criticised by Savonarola, and from 1496 Alexander strove to bring about his downfall, succeeding two years later.

ALEXANDER SEVERUS: MARCUS AURELIUS SEVERUS ALEXANDER (A.D. 208–35), Roman emperor. The son of Gessius Marcianus and Julia Avita Mamaea, he was born at Arca Caesarea in Palestine. In 221 he was adopted by the Emperor Heliogabalus (his cousin) and created Caesar. After Heliogabalus's assassination in 222, he was proclaimed emperor. He was noted for his justice, integrity and amiable character but (doubtless because of his youth) he was very much under the influence of his mother. He had difficulty in maintaining discipline, and mutinies became frequent. In March 235 he was assassinated, together with his mother, by mutinous soldiers in Gaul, where he had gone to fight invaders from Germany.

ALFONSO V of Aragon, I of Naples (1395–1458). He became King of Aragon in 1416, and in 1420 established himself as ruler of Sicily (of which he was king by hereditary right). Queen Giovanna II of Naples then sought military assistance from him (see p. 45), and adopted him as her heir, but later changed her mind, and chose Louis III of Aragon as her successor. But Louis died in 1434, and when Giovanna died in 1435, her designated heir was Louis's brother, René, whom Alfonso overcame in February 1443, after a long war. Alfonso was a strong and enlightened ruler, and his court at Naples became a famous centre of intellectual and literary activity.

AMBOISE, GEORGES D' (1460–1510), archbishop of Rouen, cardinal and statesman. A noble with court connections (his father was chamberlain to Charles VII and Louis XI), he advanced rapidly in the Church, becoming bishop of Montauban at the age of fourteen. He became archbishop of Narbonne in March 1492, and archbishop of Rouen in August 1493. He was created cardinal in December 1498 (see p. 14). He had been intimate with the Duke of Orleans since 1491, and when the Duke became King Louis XII in 1498, Amboise was appointed his chief minister. He accompanied Louis to Italy in September 1499, and in 1500 was named lieutenant-general in Italy. After being *papabile* in the two conclaves of 1503, he was appointed papal legate in France for life. He was involved in the negotiations for the Treaties of Granada (1500), Blois (1504) and in 1508 of the League of Cambrai against Venice.

ANTIOCHUS III, called 'the Great' (c. 242–187 B.C.), King of Syria. He succeeded his brother, Seleucus III, in 223, and pursued an expansionist policy, for some years with marked success. However, he failed to realise the development of Roman power in the Eastern Mediterranean. He invaded Greece in 192, but was defeated there by the Romans at Thermopylae (191) and Magnesia (190); and after the Peace of Apamea (188), the Seleucid Empire ceased to be a threat to Roman imperialism.

APPIANI, IACOPO IV (c. 1460–1510), ruler of Piombino, a city-state on the Tuscan coast. He succeeded his father Iacopo III as ruler in March 1474. In June 1501, Piombino was attacked by Cesare Borgia's army and the papal navy. On 16 August Appiani fled, and went to France to seek the help of Louis XII but without success (since the King did not want to antagonise Pope Alexander VI). On 3 September the city surrendered. However, in August 1503, after Alexander's death, the inhabitants revolted (with Florentine help), and Appiani at once returned as ruler, being then greatly helped by the protection of Ferdinand the Catholic. He was also a rather ineffective mercenary leader, serving Siena and Florence at various periods.

ARDINGHELLI, PIETRO (1470–1526). A Florentine noble, who entered public life in 1498, the same year as M. He filled various important posts until 1504, but after that his career languished for some years, perhaps because of his strong Medici sympathies. He was personal secretary to Pope Leo X from 1514 to 1520, when he was dismissed because he was discovered to be in the pay of Alfonso, Duke of Ferrara, whom he provided with information about the papal designs on his territory. He then returned to Florence.

AURELIUS ANTONINUS, MARCUS (A.D. 121–80), Roman emperor and philosopher. He became emperor in 161, and was engaged for most of his reign in campaigns on the frontiers of the Empire. He was a philosopher of the Stoic school; his *Meditations* were written in Greek.

BAGLIONI, GIANPAOLO (c. 1470–1520), ruler of Perugia and mercenary leader; he was in the service of Florence between 1493 and 1498. He is portrayed by M. (*Disc.* I, 27) as a ruthless scoundrel, who killed his cousins and nephews in order to rule, but lacked the courage to kill Pope Julius II when he had a fine opportunity. G. De Caro (*Diz. biog. d. Italiani*, vol. 5 (1963), pp. 217–20) presents him in a better light, maintaining that the massacre of his cousins and brothers in July 1500 was carried out by Carlo and Grifonetto Baglioni (relatives of his) and Girolamo Della Penna, and that Gianpaolo was an intended victim. He escaped to Marsciano, where Vitellozzo Vitelli gave him troops, permitting him to re-enter Perugia, which he then ruled, together with his father and cousin Adriano, who was the effective ruler (Gianpaolo was mostly away on military campaigns). He was one of the most determined opponents of Cesare Borgia at the Magione meeting (October 1502), and was opposed to the reconciliation with Borgia favoured by the Orsini leaders. When Borgia attacked Perugia early in January 1503, the Baglioni fled, and returned only after Alexander's death in August 1503. In April 1506, after Julius's entry into Perugia, Baglioni ceased to hold power, but after Julius's death, in February 1513, he re-established his position there. In 1511 (with Julius's permission), he began to command the Venetian army, which he continued to do until 1515. Then Pope Leo X insisted that he lead the papal army. Later Leo suspected him of treachery, and repeatedly recalled him to Rome. In March 1520 Baglioni finally came, furnished with a safe-conduct from the Pope and the strongest reassurances about his safety. Nevertheless, he was imprisoned in Castel S. Angelo, and beheaded on 11 June.

BENTIVOGLIO, ANNIBALE I (1413–45), ruler of Bologna. In 1441 he married Donnina Visconti, daughter of Duke Filippo, by whom he had one son, Giovanni II. After being a mercenary leader for some years, he became in effect the ruler of Bologna in 1443. However, his power was resented by other leading families, and on 24 June 1445 he was assassinated by Bettozzo Canetoli (not Canneschi, as M. calls him) after a baptism ceremony, to which he had been invited as a godfather.

BENTIVOGLIO, ANNIBALE II (1469–1540). Son of Giovanni II Bentivoglio, he was a mercenary leader who fought mostly for Florence. With French help, he re-entered Bologna in May 1511, together with his brother Ermes (d. 1513), but after the battle of Ravenna (April 1512) he was driven out, and exiled to Ferrara, where he died.

BENTIVOGLIO, GIOVANNI II (1443–1508), ruler of Bologna. Son of Annibale I, he became ruler after the death of Sante Bentivoglio in 1463, whose widow, Ginevra Sforza (daughter of the ruler of Pesaro), he then married. He greatly strengthened the Bentivoglio family's position in Bologna. He maintained Sante Bentivoglio's alliance with the Medici (helping them after the Pazzi plot, 1478) and with the Sforza rulers of Milan. He helped defend Ercole d'Este of Ferrara against Venice in 1482, and he assisted Caterina Sforza Riario to reconquer Forlì, after the assassination of her husband, Girolamo, in 1488. He sent his son Ermes to the Magione meeting (October 1502), directed against Cesare Borgia, but then helped Borgia overcome the Orsini leaders. He was driven out of Bologna in November 1506 by Julius II (with French help), and died in Milan.

BENTIVOGLIO, SANTE (1426–63), ruler of Bologna. Illegitimate son of Ercole Bentivoglio, he was working in the wool industry in Florence under another name when his true identity became known to the Bolognese, after the assassination in June 1445 of Annibale I Bentivoglio, who left only a very young son (Giovanni II). Such was the popular attachment to the Bentivoglio family that Sante was asked to rule the city. Encouraged by

Cosimo de' Medici (see *Ist. fior.* VI, 10), he accepted this invitation in November 1446, and ruled Bologna effectively until his death.

BORGIA, CESARE (1475–1507), son of Cardinal Rodrigo Borgia (later Pope Alexander VI) and Vannozza Catanei. Since the Cardinal had an elder son, Pedro Luiz (c. 1468–88), whom he directed towards a secular career (he was created Duke of Gandía in 1485), an ecclesiastical career was planned for Cesare. He received various benefices while still very young, and between 1489 and 1492 studied at Perugia and Pisa Universities, gaining a degree in canon and civil law. In August 1492 he was made archbishop of Valencia (replacing his father, who was now Pope) and in September 1493 he was created a cardinal.

After Pedro Luiz died in 1488, the title Duke of Gandía had passed to Cesare's younger brother, Juan. But when Juan was mysteriously murdered in June 1497, Cesare renounced his ecclesiastical offices and status (he was merely a deacon). In October 1498 he travelled to France, where he received from King Louis XII (who wanted the Pope to annul his marriage) the title of Duke of Valentinois (and so he became known in Italy as the Duke Valentino), and married Charlotte d'Albret, the niece of the King of Navarre, in May 1499. Cesare returned to Italy in September 1499 (without his pregnant wife, whom he never saw again). With the favour and help of the French King and of his father the Pope, he set out to make himself a ruler, and began to campaign in the Romagna, attacking first Imola and Forlì. For Machiavelli's account of Cesare's career, see pp. 23–9. In 1499 Alexander had appointed Cesare captain-general of the papal army; formally in his campaigns he acted as the Pope's agent, driving out the various rulers who, because of the past weaknesses of popes, had established themselves in the Papal States. However, his aim, and that of Alexander, was that he should become a powerful, independent ruler. Here it should be noted that, in Chapter VII, Machiavelli sometimes speaks of Alexander as acting when in fact it was Cesare who acted, and vice versa. This is doubtless because he saw them as having the same end in view.

After Alexander's death in August 1503, Cesare's position became extremely difficult. He attempted to secure the favour of Julius II (elected pope on 31 October 1503) but Julius, who had long been very hostile to the Borgias, was certainly not disposed to help Cesare, whatever promises he may have made. In May 1504 Cesare fled to Naples, where he was soon arrested by Gonzalo Fernandez de Còrdoba, the Spanish viceroy, and on 20 August sent to Spain, where he was imprisoned. In October 1506 he escaped and entered the service of the King of Navarre. He was killed by Navarrese rebels in a battle on 12 March 1507; he was thirty-two.

BORGIA, RODRIGO: *see* Alexander VI.

CANTACUZENE: JOHN VI or V, surnamed CANTACUZENE (c. 1292–1383), Byzantine emperor. He was born in Constantinople, and was connected with the house of Palaelogus through his mother. During Andronicus III's reign (1328–41) he was the leading official; he then became regent, and guardian of Andronicus's nine-year-old son, John Palaelogus. But powerful men at court at once opposed his rule, and he was distrusted by the Empress. He rebelled, and had himself crowned emperor in Thrace. A civil war followed, which Cantacuzene won in 1347, largely through Turkish help. He was overthrown by John Palealogus in 1354, and retired to a monastery, where he wrote a contemporary history, a commentary on Aristotle's *Ethics* and several theological works.

CARACALLA: MARCUS AURELIUS ANTONINUS, called CARACALLA or CARACALLUS (A.D. 188–217), Roman emperor. Elder son of the Emperor Septimius Severus, he was created Caesar in 196, and Augustus in 198. He and his brother Geta (created Augustus in 209) accompanied their father to Britain in 209. After his death at York in 211, the brothers returned to Rome as co-emperors. But in 212 Caracalla murdered Geta. In the same year he granted Roman citizenship to all free inhabitants of the Empire, though his motive was apparently to increase the revenues obtained from the inheritance tax. A warlike ruler, who spent much of his reign campaigning, he was killed near Carrhae in April 217 by the prefect of the praetorian guard, Opellius Macrinus, who then became emperor.

CARMAGNOLA, Count of: FRANCESCO BUSSONE (c. 1385–1432), mercenary leader. Born at Carmagnola in Piedmont. A man of humble origins, he began his military career very young, fighting with Facino Cane's forces until 1412. Then, for thirteen years, he served Duke Filippo of Milan faithfully and well. He was appointed commander of the Milanese armies in 1416, and his many successes earned him a great reputation. The Duke appointed him governor of Genoa in 1422; but he soon began to feel increasingly distrusted and little used. In 1425 he fled to Venice, and was appointed their commander in February 1426. However, he achieved much less for Venice than he had for Milan. This was doubtless partly because he was now confronted by better generals; but his desire to possess a state of his own may well have contributed to his lack of zeal. He still maintained some contacts with Duke Filippo, and the Venetians decided that they had to kill him. He was recalled to Venice for consultations; arriving there on 7 April 1432, he was arrested, charged with treason, and beheaded in St Mark's Square on 5 May.

CASAVECCHIA, FILIPPO (b. 1472, d. after 1520). A Florentine, and a close friend of M., he was one of the first readers of *The Prince* (see p. 94). He filled one or two minor public offices, and was engaged in trade, perhaps silk.

CHARLES VII, King of France (1403–61). His father, Charles VI, died in 1422, but his power was not firmly established until 1444. In 1453 the Hundred Years War ended, and the only English possession left in France was Calais. Charles is praised by M. (see p. 50) for having provided a proper basis for the French army: the royal *ordonnances* of 1445 and 1446 established a permanent cavalry force, and the *ordonnance* of 1448 an infantry force of archers.

CHARLES VIII, King of France (1470–98). The only son of Louis XI, he succeeded his father in 1483, but did not become the effective ruler until 1492. He invaded Italy in September 1494, intent on conquering the Kingdom of Naples (to which he asserted the Angevin claim), and encouraged by Ludovico Sforza, who planned to seize some Venetian territory. His armies met with little resistance, and in May 1495 he was crowned King of Naples. However, the formation of an Italian League (including Milan) compelled him to return north; at the battle of Fornovo, on the Taro river (July 1495), a much larger Italian army failed to inflict a decisive defeat on the French army, which was able to return to France.

CIOCCHI DAL MONTE or DA MONTESANSAVINO, ANTONIO MARIA, Cardinal (1461–1533). Auditor of the Apostolic Chamber and one of the twelve auditors (independent judges) of the Holy Rota. In 1503 he was appointed bishop of Città de Castello; later he was bishop of Albano. He was created a cardinal by Julius II in 1511. He was the uncle of Pope Julius III (1550–5).

CLEMENT VII, POPE: GIULIO DE' MEDICI (1478–1534). Illegitimate son of Giuliano de' Medici (1453–78), Lorenzo the Magnificent's brother, who was killed by the Pazzi plotters in Florence Cathedral. When his cousin Giovanni de' Medici became Pope Leo X in 1513, Giulio was appointed archbishop of Florence and created a cardinal. In 1517 he was made vice-chancellor of the Church. After the death of Lorenzo de' Medici, Duke of Urbino, in May 1519, he governed Florence until he was elected pope on 19 November 1523. He commissioned M. to write the *Istorie fiorentine* in November 1520; in May 1525, M. went to Rome to present the completed work to him.

COLLEONI, BARTOLOMEO (1400–75), mercenary leader. Born in Bergamo, of a minor noble family. After serving in the Kingdom of Naples, he was employed by Florence (1429–31), Venice (1431–42), Duke Filippo of Milan (1442–7), the Ambrosian Republic of Milan (1447–8), Venice (1448–51), Francesco Sforza, Duke of Milan (1451–4). In 1454 he was appointed commander-in-chief of the Venetian armies, remaining in this post until his death. Although he was the general of the defeated Venetian forces at the battle of Caravaggio (29 July 1448), he was considered one of the outstanding fifteenth-century Italian captains.

COLONNA, GIOVANNI, Cardinal (c. 1450/60–1508). Son of Antonio Colonna, Prince of Salerno. Created cardinal in 1480 by Sixtus IV, who then imprisoned him between June 1482 and November 1483, because of his family's hostility to Sixtus's policy during the War of Ferrara. When Charles VIII of France entered Rome in December 1494, he joined Cardinal della Rovere (later Julius II) and some other cardinals in urging the King to depose Alexander VI and to call a Council of the Church. In July 1499 he fled from Rome and did not return until after Alexander's death in August 1503.

COMMODUS, LUCIUS AELIUS AURELIUS (A.D. 161–92), Roman emperor. Elder son of the Emperor Marcus Aurelius, whom he succeeded in 180. After an attempt on his life in 182, he became very oppressive. He liked fighting gladiators and wild beasts in the arenas. In December 192 some persons whom he planned to kill learned of his intentions, and at once assassinated him.

CYRUS THE GREAT, founder of the Achaemenid Persian Empire, which he ruled from c. 559 to c. 529 B.C., though the details of his career are very uncertain. He is thought to have overcome the Medes c. 549.

DARIUS III, King of Persia (c. 380–330 B.C.). Codomannus took the name of Darius when he ascended the Persian throne in 336. When Alexander the Great invaded the Persian Empire in 333, Darius led his armies against him, but was defeated at Issus, in Northern Syria, and again at Arbela (or Gangamela) in September 331. In July 330, while he was fleeing to the Eastern provinces, he was killed by his cousin Bassus.

EPAMINONDAS (c. 418–362 B.C.), Theban general and statesman. After 379 he played a leading part in defending Thebes from the Spartans, who were decisively defeated at the battle of Leuctra (371). He died of wounds in the battle of Mantinea, in which the Thebans were victorious.

ESTE, ALFONSO I D', Duke of Ferrara (1476–1534). Son of Ercole I, whom he succeeded in 1505. In 1491 he married Anna Sforza, daughter of Galeazzo Maria, late Duke of Milan. She died in 1497, and in 1502 he married Lucrezia Borgia, daughter of Pope Alexander VI. He managed to preserve his power, despite the efforts of three popes (Julius II, Leo X, Clement VIII) to deprive him of his territories or to depose him, by means of excommunication and interdict as well as by force of arms, and during Clement's pontificate he succeeded in recapturing Reggio (1523) and Modena (1527).

ESTE, ERCOLE I D', Duke of Ferrara (1431–1505). He became ruler of Ferrara in 1471. Between 1482 and 1484, Ferrara was engaged in a war with the Venetians (who were supported by Sixtus IV), arising from a dispute about the salt monopoly. By the Peace of Bagnolo (1484), Ferrara ceded the Polesine district to Venice. His court was a noted cultural centre: the poet Boiardo was his minister, and he was the patron of the poet Ariosto. His daughter Isabella married Gian Francesco Gonzaga, the Marquis of Mantua; another daughter, Beatrice, married Ludovico Sforza.

EUFFREDUCCI, OLIVIERO or OLIVEROTTO (c. 1475–1502). Born at Fermo, in the Marches; after his father's early death, he was brought up by his maternal uncle, Giovanni Fogliani. In 1495 he trained as a soldier under Paulo Vitelli, and fought with him at Pisa and then in the Kingdom of Naples, on the French side. In 1497 he was employed by Fermo in the war against Ascoli, after which he returned to fight with Paulo Vitelli. When the Florentines executed Vitelli in October 1499, for treachery in the war against Pisa, Oliverotto served in Vitellozzo Vitelli's army, which was employed by Cesare Borgia in various campaigns. However, in December 1501 Oliverotto treacherously seized power in Fermo (see pp. 31–3). After further military service for Borgia in May 1502, in October he joined the Magione plotters, who wanted to curb Borgia's growing power. A feigned reconciliation took place, and then Borgia trapped Oliverotto and the other Orsini leaders at Senigallia; on 31 December 1502, he was strangled there, together with Vitellozzo Vitelli. According to the contemporary historian, Jacopo Nardi, they were strangled back to back with the same cord.

FABIUS MAXIMUS: QUINTUS FABIUS MAXIMUS, surnamed CUNCTATOR (c. 275–203 B.C.). Consul five times, he rallied the Romans after several severe defeats by Hannibal. He was famous for the cautious and effective tactics he used against Hannibal, and he opposed Scipio's plan of carrying the war to Africa. (For M.'s comments on his character and tactics, see *Disc.* III, 9.)

FERDINAND II of Aragon, and V of Castile and Leon, called 'the Catholic' (1452–1516). He married his cousin, Isabella of Castile, in 1469, and on the death of her brother, Henry IV, they become joint sovereigns of Castile. (She died in 1504.) Ferdinand became King of Aragon in 1479, on his father's death. He then launched his attack on the Moslem Kingdom of Granada, which he conquered in January 1492. For M.'s account of his character and career, see pp. 76–7. In November 1500 he made the secret Treaty of Granada with Louis XII of France: they agreed to conquer the Kingdom of Naples (ruled by Ferdinand's cousin, Frederick I) and divide it between them. Later they quarrelled and, by 1504, the French forces had been driven out, and the Kingdom of Naples annexed to Spain.

FLAMINIUS: see TITUS QUINTUS

FORTEBRACCIO, ANDREA, also known as BRACCIO DA MONTONE (1368–1424), mercenary leader and ruler. Born in Perugia, he was one of the most famous Italian mercenaries of his times. In 1416 he seized power in Perugia, and then also ruled several neighbouring towns. He was employed as general of the papal armies; he was defeated in the battle of Aquila by a Neapolitan army led by Francesco Sforza and Jacopo Caldora, and died soon afterwards from wounds. His forces, known as the 'Bracceschi', were afterwards commanded by Niccolò Piccinino (d. 1444) and Niccolò Fortebraccio (d. 1435).

FREDERICK I of Aragon, King of Naples (1452–1504). Second son of King Ferdinand I of Naples, in October 1496 he succeeded his nephew Ferdinand II, who had died without an heir. He was well regarded by his subjects, but became the victim of the secret Treaty of Granada (November 1500), by which Ferdinand the Catholic (his cousin) and Louis XII of France agreed to conquer the Kingdom of Naples and divide it between them. Louis XII's forces attacked the Kingdom from the north in the summer of 1501, and Spanish forces sent by Ferdinand (under Gonzalo Fernandez de Còrdoba) landed in Calabria in July, and occupied most of the southern part of the Kingdom within two months. Frederick was unable to resist these attacks, and in August lost his throne. He was given a safe-conduct to France, where he died in September 1504.

GIORDANI, ANTONIO (1459–1530). Born in Venafro, near Cassino, he was a lawyer, and taught for some years at Siena University. Later he was the trusted adviser of Pandolfo Petrucci, ruler of Siena (1487–1512). He represented Petrucci at the anti-Borgia meeting at Magione in October 1502.

GIOVANNA II (1371–1435), Queen of Naples. She was the widow of William, son of Leopold III of Austria, and became queen after the death of her brother Ladislao (King of Naples, 1386–1414). She led a dissolute life, having a succession of lovers and favourites, and her weakness resulted in near anarchy throughout her reign. The action of Muzio Attendolo Sforza, referred to by M. (p. 45), supporting the claim to the succession of Louis III of Anjou, against the wishes of Giovanna, and her favourite Giovanni Caracciolo, was undertaken to restore his own position in the Neapolitan kingdom. It was then that Giovanna appealed to Alfonso of Aragon for help, promising to make him her heir, but his subsequent actions led her to change her mind. She then nominated Louis as her successor; after his death in 1434, she chose his brother René.

GONZAGA, GIAN FRANCESCO, Marquis of Mantua (1466–1519), mercenary leader and ruler. He succeeded his father, Federico, in 1484. In 1490 he married Isabella d'Este, daughter of the Duke of Ferrara, who was a noted patron of the arts. He commanded the Venetian armies between 1489 and 1498, and led the forces of the Italian League against Charles VIII at the battle of Fornovo (July 1495). He later served Louis XII of France, Florence and Julius II.

GRACCHI THE, M. refers (p. 36) to TIBERIUS SEMPRONIUS GRAC-CHUS (163–133 B.C.) and his brother GAIUS SEMPRONIUS GRACCHUS (153–121 B.C.). Both brothers were tribunes of the plebs and prominent advocates of agrarian reform, and both died violent deaths in riots instigated by their aristocratic opponents.

HANNIBAL (247–c. 183 B.C.), Carthaginian general and statesman. Son of Hamilcar Barca, a noted general, he became commander-in-chief of the Carthaginian armies in 221. For three years he campaigned successfully in Spain, and in 218 he crossed the Alps and entered Italy, where he won several famous victories against Roman armies. In 204, however, Scipio attacked Carthage, and in the autumn of 203 Hannibal was recalled to Africa. His army was decisively defeated at Zama in 202. He was then appointed 'suffete' or chief magistrate of Carthage, which began to prosper again. But the Romans demanded that Hannibal be surrendered to them. He fled from Carthage to Tyre, then to Ephesus, then to Crete, and finally to Bithynia, where he took poison in order to avoid falling into the hands of the Romans.

HAWKWOOD, SIR JOHN (c. 1320–94), English mercenary leader, known to Italians as GIOVANNI ACUTO or AUCUT. Born in Essex, he is thought to have served in France under Edward III, and was probably knighted by him. He arrived in Italy with his troops, known as the White Company, about 1360. In 1364 he was the Pisan general in its war with Florence; later he served with the papal and the Milanese armies. (He married Donnina, illegitimate daughter of Bernabò Visconti, ruler of Milan, in 1377.) In 1380 he was employed by Florence, which he served faithfully until his retirement (except between December 1386 and August 1387, when he fought for Francesco Carrara, Marquis of Padua). Most of his campaigns were defensive in character, but he was considered a very able general. Florence granted him citizenship, and gave him a generous pension and tax exemption for life. He was given a state funeral. In 1436 Paolo Uccello painted a fresco of him, which is in Florence Cathedral.

HELIOGABALUS or ELAGABALUS (c. A.D. 205–22), Roman emperor. Born Varius Avitus Bassianus, he took his name from Elah-Gahal (the sun-god of Emesa, in Syria), of whom he was the hereditary priest. He was primarily interested in religion. Emperor from 218 until 222, when he was killed by the praetorian guard.

HIERO (OR HIERON) II (c. 308–216 B.C.), ruler of Syracuse. Illegitimate son of a Syracusan noble, he was appointed commander of the Syracusan army, after Pyrrhus's departure from Sicily. He decisively defeated the Mamertines (from Mamertina; formerly Messana, now Messina), who had been attacking Syracuse, and in 270 he was chosen to be King of Syracuse by the people. In 264 his forces attacked the Mamertines, who appealed to Rome for help. Hiero then allied himself with Hanno, the Carthaginian general who was then campaigning in Sicily, but after being defeated by a Roman army, he withdrew to Syracuse. In 263 he agreed to become an ally of the Romans, who recognised his right to rule South-Eastern Sicily. He remained their ally until his death.

INNOCENT VIII, POPE: GIOVANNI BATTISTA CIBO (1432–92). Born in Genoa. He was elected pope in August 1484. He had two illegitimate children when he was a young man, and he continued the nepotistic practices of his predecessor, Sixtus IV. He was succeeded by Alexander VI.

JASON. Legendary Greek hero, son of Aeson (King of Ioleus in Thessaly), and leader of the Argonauts.

JULIANUS: MARCUS DIDIUS SALVIUS JULIANUS (d. A.D. 193), Roman emperor. The son of a general, he became emperor after the assassination of Pertinax, when the praetorian guards offered the imperial throne to the highest bidder. He ruled for only two months (28 March–2 June 193): he was executed by order of the senate, and replaced by Septimius Severus.

JULIUS II, POPE: GIULIANO DELLA ROVERE (1443–1513). A nephew of Pope Sixtus IV, he too became a Franciscan; when his uncle became pope (in 1471), he was created a cardinal. From 1480 to 1482 he served as legate *a latere* to France. He was never a friend of Cardinal Rodrigo Borgia, whom he successfully opposed in the 1484 conclave. Consequently, he was out of favour during Alexander VI's pontificate; indeed, he was mostly absent from Rome (for two periods in France). He was elected pope in October 1503, after the very brief pontificate of Pius III. Julius was very much less inclined to nepotism than most recent popes (for which M. praises him: see p. 41). He lacked prudence; but his impetuosity, energy and determination made him very formidable. One of his aims was to restore order in the Papal States, and expel the rulers who were flourishing in them (e.g., Baglioni in Perugia, Bentivoglio in Bologna). In 1509 he joined the Emperor Maximilian and Louis XII of France in their attack on Venice (which had refused to give up some territories in the Romagna, taken in 1503). Afterwards, when the French power seemed too great, he formed an alliance with Venice and Spain, and in 1511 he attacked the Duke of Ferrara (who supported the French), but without success (see pp. 6, 48). Although the Holy League's forces were defeated at Ravenna (April 1512), the intervention of Swiss forces resulted in a French withdrawal from Italy (see p. 48). Julius was a noted patron of the arts, giving work to Michelangelo and Raphael; and the new St Peter's Basilica, designed by Bramante, was begun during his pontificate.

JULIUS CAESAR (100–44 B.C.). His notable liberality made him very popular, and contributed markedly to his early political successes, before he won glory as a general. After his victory over Pompey in the civil war, and his return to Rome in 45, he was the master of Rome. He was assassinated in March 44.

LEO X, POPE: GIOVANNI DE' MEDICI (1475–1521). Second son of Lorenzo the Magnificent, he studied theology and canon law at Pisa

University (1489–91), and was made a cardinal by Innocent VIII in 1492. He did not vote for Alexander VI in the conclave in August 1492, and then went to live in Florence; after the fall of the Medici in 1494, he lived abroad, returning to Rome in 1500. In October 1511, Julius II appointed him legate of Bologna and the Romagna. He was elected pope in March 1513. He presided over the Fifth Lateran Council (called by Julius II in May 1512), which ended in 1517. In 1516 Leo negotiated a concordat with Francis I, which regulated Church–State relations in France until 1789. In 1517 Cardinal Alfonso Petrucci and some other cardinals attempted to poison Leo. Petrucci was executed and the other cardinals were heavily fined. In the same year, Luther attacked various abuses in the Church; after attempts to silence Luther, Leo condemned him in a bull issued in June 1520. Luther publicly burned the bull in December, and Leo excommunicated him in January 1521. In September 1521 Leo conferred the title of Defender of the Faith on Henry VIII for his book against Luther. Leo was a very generous patron of humanists and artists; he gave much work to Raphael.

LOUIS IX, King of France (1214–70). He succeeded his father, Louis VIII, in 1226. He went on two crusades, during the second of which he died; he was canonised in 1297. He is credited with having instituted the *parlement* of Paris about 1254.

LOUIS XI, King of France (1423–83), son of Charles VII and Marie of Anjou. He became king in 1461. He added Burgundy, Franche Comté, Picardy and Artois to the territory of the French crown. M. criticises him (see p. 50) for having disbanded the French cavalry, and for employing Swiss troops, which he began to do in 1474.

LOUIS XII, King of France (1462–1515). He was the Duke of Orleans before becoming king in 1498. When Charles VIII invaded Italy in 1494, he commanded the forces that occupied Genoa, and he remained in Northern Italy while Charles went southwards. After his marriage to Queen Jeanne was annulled by Alexander VI in 1499 (see p. 14), he married Anne of Brittany, widow of Charles VIII. In September 1499 he invaded Lombardy (asserting his claim, deriving from his Visconti connections, to the Duchy of Milan), and for most of his reign he was a powerful figure in Italy, except for the Kingdom of Naples, where his armies had been defeated by the Spaniards (see pp. 7, 11–14, 27).

MACRINUS, MARCUS OPELLIUS SEVI RUS (c. A.D. 164–218), Roman emperor. Born in Mauretania, North Africa, he became praetorian prefect under Caracalla, whom he succeeded as emperor in April 217. But his reign was very short: in June 218 he was killed near Antioch.

MALATESTA, PANDOLFO V (1475–1534), ruler of Rimini. Illegitimate son of Roberto Malatesta whom he succeeded in 1482, Galeotto Malatesta acting as regent for ten years. In 1493 Rimini was placed under Venetian protection for two years by Elisabetta, Pandolfo's mother. A violent and oppressive ruler, he narrowly escaped being assassinated in January 1498, and lost Venetian support. He was thus ill-placed to resist Cesare Borgia's attack, and in October 1500 he left for Bologna. In October 1502 he recaptured power (but only for a month), again in May 1522 (for nine months) and finally in 1527 (for six months). He was the last Malatesta ruler of Rimini.

MANFREDI, ASTORRE (or ASTORGIO) III (1485–1502), ruler of Faenza, which had been ruled by the Manfredi family since the beginning of the fourteenth century (though there were intervals of republican government and rule by papal legates). Son of Galeotto Manfredi and Francesca Bentivoglio (daughter of Giovanni II, ruler of Bologna), he became ruler at the age of three, after his father was assassinated on 31 May 1488. Faenza was attacked by Cesare Borgia on 10 November 1500, but Manfredi put up a stiff resistance. He was a popular ruler, and was supported by Florence and Giovanni Bentivoglio, his grandfather. At the onset of winter, Borgia abandoned the siege; but he attacked Faenza again on 7 March 1501. Within six weeks the inhabitants were starving, and the city surrendered on 25 April. Contrary to the terms of the surrender, Astorre and his younger brother were taken to Rome, where they were imprisoned in Castel Sant'Angelo. They were strangled there in January 1502, and Astorre's body was found in the Tiber on 9 June. He was the last Manfredi ruler of Faenza.

MAXIMILIAN I, EMPEROR (1459–1519). He was elected King of the Romans, or German King, in 1485; in August 1493 his father, the Emperor Frederick III, died, and he became sole ruler of Germany and head of the Habsburg family. In March 1494 he married Bianca Maria, daughter of Galeazzo Sforza, late Duke of Milan. In February 1508 he assumed the title of Roman Emperor Elect, Pope Julius II giving his consent. He died in January 1519, and was succeeded by his grandson, Charles V. M., who visited his court in 1508, considered him an indecisive ruler (see p. 82).

MAXIMINUS, GAIUS JULIUS VERUS (d. A.D. 238), Roman emperor. A

Thracian centurion of peasant stock, he was made emperor by the soldiers in 235, after Alexander Severus had been assassinated. He continued campaigning in Germany and on the Danube until 238, when the proclamation of Gordian I and his son as emperors moved Maximinus to invade Italy. He was killed by his troops before he reached Rome, during the siege of Aquileia.

MEDICI, GIOVANNI DE': *see* LEO X

MEDICI, GIULIANO DE', Duke of Nemours (1479–1516), third son of Lorenzo the Magnificent. After his brother's election as Pope Leo X in March 1513, he lived mostly in Rome. M. originally intended to dedicate *The Prince* to him (see p. 94).

MEDICI, GIULIO DE': *see* CLEMENT VII.

MEDICI, LORENZO DE', 'the Magnificent' (1449–1492), son of Piero, and grandson of Cosimo. After Piero's death in 1469, Lorenzo and his brother Giuliano became the leading citizens of Florence; and after Giuliano was killed by the Pazzi conspirators in 1478, Lorenzo's primacy was uncontested. He rather neglected the family banking business, devoting himself to government and politics, as well as to patronage of the arts and letters (and he was himself a notable writer of verse and other literary works).

MEDICI, LORENZO DE', Duke of Urbino (1492–1519), son of Piero de' Medici (1471–1503; ruler of Florence, 1492–4), and grandson of Lorenzo the Magnificent. *The Prince* is dedicated to him. In May 1516, at Leo X's instigation, he drove Duke Francesco Maria della Rovere out of Urbino; Leo created him Duke of Urbino and ruler of Pesaro, and appointed him *gonfaloniere* of the Church. He was the father of Alessandro (1510–37; first Duke of Florence, 1530–7) and Catherine (1519–89), wife of Henry II of France.

MEDICI, PIERO DE' (1471–1503), the eldest son of Lorenzo the Magnificent. After his father's death in 1492, he was ruler of Florence until November 1494, when he was exiled. He died in the battle of Garigliano (December 1503), fighting for the French against the Spaniards.

MONTEFELTRO, GUIDO UBALDO, Duke of Urbino (1472–1508). He succeeded his father Federico (a famous mercenary, ruler and patron of the arts) in 1482. He lacked his father's military skill, but his court was a noted centre of art and learning. Castiglione was at Urbino for some years, and his *Cortegiano* (1528) is set in that court. Guido Ubaldo was suddenly attacked by Cesare Borgia on 21 June 1502, and he fled, going first to Ravenna and then to Mantua. He returned after the Magione meeting, on 29 October, and destroyed the fortresses at Gubbio and Pergola; but early in January 1503, alarmed by the Senigallia killings, he fled to Venice, returning to Urbino only after Alexander VI's death in August 1503. He was succeeded by his nephew, Francesco Maria della Rovere.

MOSES. The lawgiver and prophet, who led the Israelites from captivity in Egypt to the borders of the Promised Land.

NABIS (c. 240–192 B.C.), ruler of Sparta. He seized power in 207, and followed an expansionist policy. However, he suffered several reverses at the hands of the Romans and Philopoemen, leader of the Achaean League. He was assassinated in an uprising in Sparta.

ORCO, REMIRRO DE: RAMIRO DE LORQUA (d. 1502). A Spaniard, he accompanied Cesare Borgia to the French court in 1498. Borgia appointed him governor of the Romagna in 1501, and had him killed at Cesena on 26 December 1502 (see p. 26).

ORSINI, GIOVAN BATTISTA, Cardinal (c. 1465?–1503). Son of Lorenzo and Clarice Orsini, he received many benefices while still very young. He was created a cardinal in 1483 by Sixtus IV. He supported Rodrigo Borgia's election as Pope Alexander VI in 1492, and received many favours from him. But later he opposed Cesare Borgia's ambitious schemes (he was present at the Magione meeting in October 1502). After an agreement with Borgia, in January 1503 he returned to Rome, where he was immediately imprisoned, and then poisoned on 23 February. (Paulo Orsini and Francesco Orsini, the Duke of Gravina, captured by Borgia in Senigallia on 31 December 1502, were not strangled until 18 January 1503, when it was heard that Cardinal Orsini had been taken.)

ORSINI, NICCOLÒ, Count of Pitigliano (1442–1510). A mercenary leader who at various times fought for the Papacy, Florence (distinguishing himself at the battle of Campomorto in 1482) and the Papacy again. In 1495 he entered the service of Venice, in which he remained until his death. He was their leader at the battle of Vailà (or Agnadello) in 1509; M. emphasises that this defeat spelt the ruin of Venetian power. He was the cousin of Paulo Orsini, killed by Cesare Borgia in 1503.

ORSINI, PAULO (c. 1460–1503). Illegitimate son of Cardinal Latino Orsini, he distinguished himself with the papal troops in the war of Ferrara in 1483. He fought at various times for the Florentines and the Venetians and, later, for the papal armies and those of Cesare Borgia. He was one of the leading figures in the Magione plot in 1502, and then defeated Micheletto, Borgia's general, near Colmazzo. He represented the Orsini faction at the reconciliation meeting with Borgia at Imola (see p. 25), but together with the other leaders was tricked by him at Senigallia in December 1502; he was held prisoner at the Castel della Pieve where, on 18 January 1503, he was strangled with his cousin Francesco Orsini, Duke of Gravina.

PALAELOGUS: JOHN V or VI, surnamed PALAELOGUS (1332–91), Byzantine emperor. Son of Emperor Andronicus III, whom he succeeded in 1341; his supporters fought for six years against John Cantacuzene, his guardian, who at first acted as regent but soon had himself crowned emperor. John Palaelogus overcame Cantacuzene in 1354, but his reign was unhappy; his son rebelled against him, and the Turks encroached on his kingdom to such an extent that he became their tributary in 1381.

PERTINAX, PUBLIUS HELVIUS (A.D. 126–93), Roman emperor. The son of a charcoal-burner, he was born in Liguria. He held many important posts, both civil and military (he was a general in Raetia and in Britain). After the assassination of Commodus, he was proclaimed emperor by the praetorian guard on 1 January 193. But his attempts to impose strict discipline antagonised the soldiers, who mutinied and killed him on 28 March 193.

PETRUCCI, PANDOLFO (1450–1512), ruler of Siena. A rich merchant, he was exiled from Siena for many years. He returned in 1487, became leader of the Noveschi faction and, with his brother Jacopo, succeeded in seizing power. (Jacopo died in 1497.) He was an adroit and ruthless man. (He killed his father-in-law, Niccolò Borghese, because he was opposed to Petrucci's policy of peace with Florence, with which Siena had been at war over the possession of Montepulciano.) But he was greatly helped by having Antonio Giordani as his minister (see p. 80). Petrucci was hostile to Cesare Borgia, and sent Giordani as his representative to the Magione meeting (October 1502). When attacked by Borgia's forces in January 1503, he fled to Lucca. But at the end of March, he was restored to power, being helped by Louis XII; the Florentines consented to this, because Petrucci promised to restore Montepulciano to them. He died in May 1512, and was succeeded by his son Borghese.

PHILIP II, King of Macedon (382–336 B.C.). He became King of Macedon in 359, and laid the foundations of Macedonian power in Greece on which his son Alexander was to build. (For M.'s condemnation of his methods, see *Disc.* I, 26). He was assassinated in 336. (For M.'s discussion of the reason, see *Disc.* II, 28.)

PHILIP V, King of Macedon (238–179 B.C.). He became king in 221. He was involved in several wars against the Romans. He was heavily defeated at sea in 215, but then attacked Illyria by land. In 207, the Romans and various Greek states attacked him, but he resisted successfully. In 200, the Romans again attacked him, and in 197 Flaminius decisively defeated his army at Cynoscephalae in Thessaly.

PHILIP IV (called *le Bel* or 'the Fair'), King of France (1268–1314). He became king in 1285. He was involved in a long struggle with Pope Boniface VIII. In 1307 he attacked the Templars.

PHILOPOEMEN (253–184 B.C.), Greek general. He was born at Magapolis. After spending eleven years as a mercenary in Crete, he was appointed commander of the Achaean League cavalry in 211, and general of all the League's forces in 208. He defeated Nabis, the ruler of Sparta, several times. He was executed, after being captured during a revolt at Messene.

PIUS III, POPE: FRANCESCO TODESCHINI PICCOLOMINI (1439–1503). Nephew of Pius II, who created him cardinal in 1460. He had an untainted reputation but was already very ill when elected pope on 22 September 1503, in succession to Alexander VI. He died on 18 October, and was succeeded by Julius II.

PYRRHUS, King of Epirus, in North-Western Greece (c. 318–272 B.C.). He was a very fine general who, after 280, campaigned against the Romans in Italy, and the Carthaginians in Sicily. He won several victories, but at great cost (hence the phrase 'a Pyrrhic victory').

RIARIO, GIROLAMO, Count (1443–88), ruler of Imola and Forlì. Favoured by his uncle (or perhaps father), Pope Sixtus IV, he became ruler of Imola in 1473 and of Forlì in 1480. In 1477 he married Caterina Sforza, daughter of Galeazzo Maria Sforza, Duke of Milan. He commanded the papal troops in the war of Ferrara (1482–4). His involvement in the Pazzi plot (1478) aroused the unrelenting hostility of Lorenzo de' Medici, who tried to undermine his power. His oppressive rule antagonised his subjects and he was assassinated in Forlì on 14 April 1488.

RIARIO, RAFFAELLO, Cardinal (c. 1452–1521). He was the son of Valentina Riario (niece of Sixtus IV) and Antonio Sansoni, but was called Riario. Sixtus made him a cardinal in 1477. On 26 April 1478 he was celebrating Mass in the Florence Cathedral when the unsuccessful Pazzi attack on the Medici brothers was made, and was lucky to escape with his life. He was archbishop of Pisa from 1479 until 1499, and he also held several other ecclesiastical offices. During Alexander VI's pontificate he avoided Rome, but flourished under that of his uncle Julius II.

ROMULUS and his brother REMUS were the mythical founders of Rome.

SANSEVERINO, ROBERTO DA, Count of Caiazzo (1418–87), mercenary leader. The illegitimate son of a Neapolitan baron, he fought for Francesco and Galeazzo Sforza, and also for Ludovico Sforza, who gave him the town of Tortona in 1479. In 1482 he became the Venetian commander in the war against Ferrara. After 1484 he commanded the papal forces in the war against Naples. Then he returned to the service of Venice, and was killed in the battle of Calliano, in Trent, fighting against the army of Sigismund, Duke of Austria.

SAVONAROLA, GIROLAMO (1452–98). Born in Ferrara, of a prosperous family. His grandfather, Michele Savonarola (1384–1468), who was Niccolò d'Este's physician and wrote medical works, helped to educate him; and he studied medicine for two years before going to Bologna and entering the Dominican order, in 1474. After completing his theological studies at Ferrara in 1482, he was sent to Florence, where he stayed until 1487. He then preached in Ferrara, S. Gimignano, Brescia, Genoa and other towns. He returned to Florence in 1490. His prophetic sermons made a great impression: he predicted the imminent deaths of Lorenzo de' Medici, Pope Innocent VIII and the King of Naples; he also denounced the moral laxity and worldliness of the Florentines, and the evil ways of the papal court. After the departure of Piero de' Medici, in November, 1494, Savonarola, the prior of S. Marco, became the most influential man in Florence. Some people resented the new austere ways, and the Medici party made difficulties; but the most important reason for his downfall was Alexander VI's hostility towards this implacable critic of abuses in the Church. Savonarola was excommunicated and an interdict on Florence was threatened; his popularity waned and the 'unarmed prophet' (as M. calls him, p. 21) was hanged, and his body burned, in the Piazza della Signoria in May 1498. He greatly valued republican liberty, and wrote a short political treatise as well as several spiritual works.

SCALI, GIORGIO (c. 1350–1382). He emerged as a leader during the

Ciompi uprising in Florence (1378), but was held to have abused his power, and was beheaded in January 1382.

SCIPIO: PUBLIUS CORNELIUS SCIPIO AFRICANUS (c. 236–183 B.C.), Roman general. He distinguished himself during and after the disastrous defeat at Cannae in 216. In 210 he was appointed leader of the Roman armies in Spain, and by 207 he had driven out the Carthaginians. In 204 he led the Roman invasion of North Africa, and won a great victory against Hannibal's army at Zama in October 202. After Carthage's submission in 201, Scipio returned to Rome in triumph, and the surname Africanus was conferred on him.

SEVERUS, LUCIUS SEPTIMIUS (A.D. 146–211), Roman emperor. Born on the North African coast, he went to Rome as a young man. In 172 he became quaestor and senator. After the assassination of the Emperor Pertinax in 193, the praetorian guards sold the throne to Didius Julianus, who proved very ineffectual. Pescennius Niger in Syria and Clodius Albinus in Britain were then both proclaimed emperor by their troops. Severus, who was in Illyria with his troops, marched quickly on Rome, where the senate made him emperor and put Julianus to death. Niger was defeated and killed at Issus in 194. In 196 Severus went to France, where he defeated Albinus near Lyons. He brought him to Rome as a captive and had him beheaded. Severus fought against the Parthians between 197 and 202. After a period in Rome (202–8), he went to Britain. After much campaigning, he died at York.

SFORZA, ASCANIO, Cardinal (1455–1505). Son of Francesco Sforza; a worldly and corrupt prelate, he held many benefices, including the bishopric of Pavia. He was created cardinal in 1484, and was very influential in furthering the schemes of his brother, Ludovico, ruler of Milan. He was friendly with Cardinal Rodrigo Borgia, and helped him to become Pope Alexander VI, though their relationship was later sometimes strained. In 1492 he helped arrange the marriage of Alexander's daughter, Lucrezia Borgia (1480–1519) with Giovanni Sforza, ruler of Pesaro; this marriage was annulled in 1497 for political reasons. He died of the plague.

SFORZA, FRANCESCO, Duke of Milan (1401–66). Son of Muzio Attendolo Sforza, he led the Sforza mercenary troops after his father's death in 1424. He was employed by Duke Filippo Visconti of Milan, and married his illegitimate daughter Bianca Maria in 1441. After Duke Filippo's death (1447), he served the Ambrosian republic of Milan, and defeated the Venetian forces at Caravaggio (July 1448). Then he changed sides, and led the Venetian forces against the republic of Milan. In 1550 he entered Milan as duke. He had been helped by Cosimo de' Medici, who lamented that, after becoming duke, Sforza did not want to undertake a campaign against Lucca that he had promised.

SFORZA, GIOVANNI, Count of Cotignola and ruler of Pesaro (1466–1510). Great-grandson of Muzio Attendolo Sforza, he became ruler of Pesaro on his father's death in 1483. He married Lucrezia Borgia (Alexander VI's daughter), in 1493, but Alexander annulled the marriage in December 1497, when his own policies changed. Attacked by Cesare Borgia in October 1500, he was obliged to flee. In 1503, after Alexander's death, he returned to Pesaro and in 1504 obtained a new investiture from Julius II.

SFORZA, LUDOVICO, Duke of Milan (1451–1508), known as 'il Moro' ('the Moor'), probably because of his dark hair and complexion. He was the second son of Francesco Sforza. His elder brother, Galeazzo Maria, was assassinated in December 1476, leaving a young son, Gian Galeazzo. It was not until 1480 that Ludovico succeeded in making himself regent; he then became in effect the ruler of Milan, though he became duke only in 1494, the year in which Gian Galeazzo died (perhaps by poison). He married Beatrice d'Este (1475–97), daughter of Ercole I, Duke of Ferrera, in 1491. He was a cultivated man, and a patron of the arts; Leonardo da Vinci worked in Milan, 1482–99. But he was an astute and unscrupulous ruler rather than a strong one, and he encouraged Charles VIII's invasion of Italy in 1494, hoping thereby to gain some Venetian territory. M. thought he bore a heavy responsibility for the disasters that followed (see p. 85n. and, esp., *Ist. fior.* VIII, 36). When Louis XII, claiming the Duchy of Milan, invaded Lombardy in September 1499, Ludovico quickly lost power. He regained it in February 1500 but was captured after a battle near Novara in April, and spent the rest of his life as a French prisoner, in the castle of Loches, near Tours.

SFORZA, MASSIMILIANO (1493–1530), Duke of Milan. He was the eldest son of Ludovico Sforza and Beatrice d'Este; he was Duke of Milan from 1512 until 1515, losing power after the battle of Marignano (September 1515).

SFORZA, MUZIO (from GIACOMUCCIO) ATTENDOLO (1369–1424), mercenary leader, and father of Francesco Sforza. At an early age, he took to the career of arms; he fought under Alberico da Barbiano, who gave him the surname Sforza. In 1398 he entered the service of Perugia; afterwards he fought for the Duke of Milan, Florence, the Duke of Ferrara, for Florence again, then for Ladislao, King of Naples, and Queen Giovanna, his successor. He was considered one of the ablest Italian generals.

SFORZA RIARIO, CATERINA (c. 1463–1509). Illegitimate daughter of Galeazzo Maria Sforza; a domineering and ruthless woman, she possessed the most forceful characteristics of the Sforza family. She married Girolamo Riario in 1477. After his assassination in 1488, she succeeded in retaining power (assisted by Ludovico Sforza), and crushed the conspirators. But her harsh rule incurred the hatred of her subjects. Cesare Borgia captured Imola on 25 November 1499; on 15 December the people revolted against Caterina as he approached Forlì, which he captured on 19 December. Caterina held out in the fortress of Ravaldino until 12 January 1500.

SIXTUS IV, POPE: FRANCESCO DELLA ROVERE (1414–84). Born near Savona in Liguria, he joined the Franciscan order, becoming its general in 1464. He taught at several Italian universities, and wrote some theological and philosophical works; he was a noted preacher. He was created cardinal in 1467, and elected pope in August 1471. He was immediately very active in promoting a crusade, but his reign was marred by his exceptional nepotism. Giuliano della Rovere (later Julius II) was made a cardinal, as were the rascally Pietro Riario, and Raffaello Riario. Sixtus also devoted much effort to establishing Girolamo Riario as a ruler in the Romagna. These schemes involved him in conflicts with the Medici, and in the Pazzi conspiracy (1478) against them; a war with Florence followed (1478–80). Sixtus was also involved with Venice in a war against Naples (1482–84). He was a prominent patron of humanists and artists; in 1481 the building of the Sistine Chapel (named after him) was completed.

SODERINI, FRANCESCO, Cardinal (1453–1524). Brother of Piero Soderini, he was made bishop of Volterra in 1478, and cardinal in 1503 (by Alexander VI). His relations with the Medici Pope Leo X deteriorated after his alleged involvement in the plot against Leo led by Cardinal Petrucci in 1517. He fled from Rome and did not return until after Leo's death in December 1521.

SODERINI, GIOVAN BATTISTA (1484–1528). Nephew of Piero Soderini, he was exiled from Florence in 1512, when the Medici returned to power, though he was permitted to return the following year. After being involved in the 1522 anti-Medici plot, he was against expelled. However, he took part in the defence of Florence in 1527; he was captured by the Spanish troops, and taken to Spain, dying there in Burgos. (F. Gaeta.)

SODERINI, PIERO (1452–1522). Son of Tommaso Soderini, a leading adviser of Piero de' Medici (son of Cosimo) and Lorenzo the Magnificent. He became prominent in Florentine affairs in the 1480s; he was favoured by Piero de' Medici (son of Lorenzo the Magnificent, ruler of Florence, 1492–4), who in 1493 sent him as ambassador to the court of Charles VIII of France. In 1501 he was made *gonfaloniere* of Justice, and in September 1502 *gonfaloniere* for life, in effect, head of state, a new post created in August 1502, in order to make the republic more stable. He was an honest man, patient and conciliatory, and a good administrator. But M., who liked him, thought he was too weak, or insufficiently ruthless, with the Medici faction, which never accepted the new regime, and which should been crushed (see esp. *Disc.* III, 3). He had always favoured a pro-French policy, and fled from Florence as the Spanish troops approached in September 1512. He was permitted to live in Rome from early 1513 by Leo X (perhaps to placate Cardinal Francesco Soderini, Piero's brother) and he died there.

THESEUS. Legendary hero of Attica. He slew the Minotaur in the labyrinth in Crete.

TITUS, FLAVIUS SABINUS VESPASIANUS (c. A.D. 40–81), Roman emperor. Son of the Emperor Vespasian, he served with the armies in Germany, Britain and Syria. He fought together with his father in the Jewish War, and captured Jerusalem in September 70. In July 69 Vespasian had become emperor; when Titus returned to Italy in 71 he received the title of Caesar and became Vespasian's associate. He was emperor from 79 to 81, and was a generous and beneficent ruler.

TITUS QUINTUS: TITUS QUINCTIUS FLAMINIUS (c. 227–174 B.C.) In 198 he became consul, and in 197 he led the Roman army in the battle of Cynoscephalae, in Thessaly, in which Philip V of Macedon was defeated. He forced Nabis of Sparta to surrender Argos in 195, and in 193–192 led a successful attack on the Spartan ruler. In 183 he was involved in the death of Hannibal, who had taken refuge at the court of Prusias, King of Bithynia. Flaminius pressed Prusias to hand over Hannibal, but to avoid this fate the Carthaginian took poison.

VARANO, GIULIO CESARE DA (c. 1432–1502), ruler of Camerino, in the

Marches. His family had ruled Camerino since the late thirteenth century. He governed it from 1444 until 1502. In 1451 he married Giovanna Malatesta of Rimini. In July 1502 Cesare Borgia attacked the city, and captured Varano and three of his sons. After holding them in prison for some time, he had all four strangled. However, one of his sons, Giovanni Maria, had escaped Borgia's clutches; after Alexander VI's death (August 1503) and Cesare Borgia's downfall, he returned to Camerino and, assisted by his mother, ruled the city. Giovanni's position was confirmed by Julius II and Leo X; he died in 1527.

VETTORI, FRANCESCO (1474–1539). Born into a noble Florentine family, he was a close friend of M., but did little to help him in his difficulties after 1512. He was Florentine envoy to the courts of the Emperor Maximilian (1507–9) and Pope Leo X (1513–15). He wrote a *Sommario della istoria d'Italia (1511–27)* and various other pieces.

VISCONTI, BERNABÒ, (1323–85), ruler of Milan and most of Lombardy (except Pavia), 1355–85. A man of remarkable energy (he fathered at least twenty children, fourteen of whom were legitimate), he was famous for his bizarre punishments (and, less often, rewards). He was a centralising ruler, who maintained order in his dominions. But his contempt for his nephew, Gian Galeazzo Visconti, ruler of Pavia from 1378, led to his downfall: underrating Gian Galeazzo, Bernabò carelessly allowed himself to be captured by him in May 1385. He was imprisoned in the castle of Trezzo, where he died (probably poisoned) in December.

VISCONTI, FILIPPO MARIA, Duke of Milan (1392–1447). Son of Gian Galeazzo Visconti, he became Duke in 1412, after the death of his elder brother, Giovanni Maria. He enjoyed early success in recovering most of the territory ruled by his father (and lost during his brother's reign), but his expansionist policies aroused the opposition of the leading Italian powers, and he was continually involved in wars. After the Peace of Cremona (1441), his influence declined. He had no legitimate sons; in 1441 his illegitimate daughter Bianca Maria (1422–68) married Francesco Sforza, then leader of the Milanese armies.

VISCONTI, GABRIELE MARIA (d. 1408), ruler of Pisa. An illegitimate son of Gian Galeazzo Visconti (1353–1402), Duke of Milan from 1395 until 1402, he became ruler of Pisa in 1402. However, his power was never very secure, and he sold the city to the Florentines in 1405, Jean Boucicaut (c. 1366–1421), a French general, acting as intermediary. Later Boucicaut killed him.

VITELLI, NICCOLÒ (1414–86), mercenary leader and ruler of Città di Castello, in Umbria. After holding various political posts in Rome and Tuscany (where he became friendly with the Medici family), he returned to Città di Castello in 1462. He became leader of the popular faction and, after a massacre of the nobles in 1468, ruler of the city. He was driven out in 1474 by Cardinal Giuliano della Rovere (acting for Sixtus IV); in 1482 he regained power (assisted by Florence), and destroyed the fortresses that Sixtus had had built. His four sons, Giovanni, Camillo, Paulo and Vitellozzo, were mercenaries, and all met violent deaths.

VITELLI, PAULO (c. 1465–99), mercenary leader, son of Niccolò Vitelli. In 1487 Pope Innocent VIII exiled him from Città di Castello. He then fought as a mercenary, gaining such a great reputation that Florence hired him as commander of its forces in June 1498. By September 1499, however, the Florentines had became very dissatisfied with Vitelli's prosecution of the war against Pisa, and suspicious of his conduct. They arrested him and, after a short trial, beheaded him on 1 October 1499.

VITELLI, VITELLOZZO (c. 1470–1502), mercenary leader. Son of Niccolò Vitelli; he possessed much power in Città di Castello but spent most of his time fighting as a mercenary. After his brother Paulo was appointed commander of the Florentine forces (in June 1498), Vitellozzo also played an important part; and when Paulo was arrested and executed for treachery (October 1499), Vitellozzo was very lucky to escape with his life. He then fought for Cesare Borgia, and revenge seems to have been one of his motives (Borgia was no friend of Florence, and had designs on Tuscany). However, later he became alarmed by Borgia's growing power, and joined other North Italian leaders at the Magione meeting (9 October 1502). A revolt against Borgia followed, but Borgia then met Paulo Orsini, their representative (25–8 October), and pretended to be reconciled with them (see p. 25). Vitellozzo, the Orsini leaders and Oliverotto Euffreducci were tricked by Borgia at Senigallia, where Vitellozzo was strangled with Oliverotto on 31 December 1502. He was married to a daughter of Paulo Orsini.

Index of subjects[a]

ability xxxiii, 5, 8, 19–23, 28, 30, 31, 34, 40, 45, 46, 51, 64, 68, 72, 84, 87–9, 103, 104, 107
absolute regimes 37
action 20, 23, 27, 28, 53, 60, 62–4, 70–2, 79, 80, 82, 83, 85–7
adversity 34, 36, 37, 51, 54, 84
advice xxii, xxiii, 38, 62, 81, 82, 97
advisers xviii, 80–2
affability xxii, 54, 55, 79
affection xvii, 6, 74, 90, 93; see also devotion
aggression 87
agriculture 79
allegory 61
alliances 10, 12, 22, 27, 40, 79, 113
allies xv, 12, 13, 29, 36n., 54, 64, 65, 77–9, 83, 105, 113
ambition 10–13, 15, 28, 36, 42, 43, 45, 64, 66, 67
amicizia xxxiii, 113
amico xxxiii, 54n., 113
anarchy 34, 109, 110
ancient history 3, 48, 74
anger 64, 70, 82, 84, 85
animals 61
annexation 5–17, 22–9, 46, 73
appearances xix, 62, 63
appetites 35
archers 19, 104
armies: different types of 42, 43, 76, 83,

89, 90; foreign xi, xiii, 5, 22–9, 44, 50; native xi, xiii, xiv, 5, 19–22, 43, 44, 50, 51
arrogance 60, 66, 67, 84, 88
assicurare 112
assicurarsi 112, 113
authority 15, 26, 35, 44, 49, 66, 71, 97
auxiliaries xiv, 43, 48–51
avaro 55

barbarian yoke 87–91
barbarity 69
barons 15, 16, 40–2, 76
baseness 70, 104
beasts xix, xx, 61
belief 21
benefits x, 7, 11, 18, 29, 33, 34, 36, 39, 54, 56, 59, 69, 72, 87, 97
benevolence 67
betrayal 31
birth, low 70
blame xvi, 13, 54, 55, 63, 76, 84, 94, 97, 98
blood, shedding of 59, 73
boldness 87, 97
bribery 22, 56n., 105
brutality 70

calculation 87
candour 81, 82
capacity 23, 30, 44, 48, 62, 67, 80, 83, 86, 98

[a] This Index, which is fairly full but not exhaustive, registers references to subjects rather than words (except Italian words). E.g., 'despised' is included under 'contempt', 'astuteness' and 'guile' under 'cunning', and 'necessity' includes references to all the words discussed on p. 108. The verbal, adverbial, and adjectival forms are included under the appropriate nouns.

141

Index of proper names

Gracchi, the 36, 125
Granada 76
Granada, Treaty of 13n.
Greece 8, 10, 11, 17, 18, 22, 78, 83, 103
Greeks, the 48
Guelph factions 73

Hamilcar 30
Hannibal xxxiv, 60, 97, 99, 100, 106,
   125–6
Hawkwood, John 45, 126
Heaven 98
Heliogabalus 67, 71, 126
Hellespont 22
Hercules 61n.
Herodian 67n.
Hiero 22, 49, 50, 51n., 107, 126
Holy League ix, 7n.
Holy Roman Emperor 109
Holy Roman Empire 46

Imola xxv, xxvi, 49, 112
Innocent VIII 41n., 126
Ionia 22
Israelites, the 20, 88
Italians, the 14
Italian military qualities, 88–90
Italy ix, xi, xii, xiv, 11, 13, 14, 24, 40, 41,
   45–7, 49, 69, 70, 73, 83, 88–90, 97,
   99, 103

Jason 61n., 127
Jeanne de Valois 14n.
Jews, Spanish 77
Julianus 67–9, 71, 127
Julius II ix, xxvi, 6, 28, 29, 41, 48, 56,
   75n., 79, 85n., 86, 87, 97, 98, 106,
   117, 119, 127, 140
Julius Caesar 17n., 57, 127
Justinus xxxiv, 22n., 30n.

League of Cambrai 13n.
Leo X xii, 42, 118, 127–8
Lisio, Giuseppe xxxiii, xxxv, 31n.
Livy xxiv, xxxiv, 36n., 53n., 60n., 78n.
Locri 60
Lodi, Peace of 73n.
Lombardy xxxiii, 11–14, 45, 79, 88, 103
Louis IX of France 66n., 128
Louis XI of France 50, 128
Louis XII of France ix, xi, xiii, xxv, xxvi,
   xxxiii, 7, 11–14, 24, 25, 27, 40, 47, 56,
   73n., 86, 87, 108, 128

Lucca 12, 27

Macedonia, Kingdom of 10
Macrinus 67, 71, 128–9
Magione plot 25
Magnesia, battle of 10n.
Malatesta, Pandolfo 12n., 129
Mamaea, Julia Avita 68n.
Mamertines, the 22n.
Manfredi, Astorre 12n., 129
Mantua 12
Marlowe, Christopher 107n.
Maximilian I ix, xxiii, xxvi, 73n., 82, 129
Maximinus 67, 68, 70, 71, 129–30
Medes, the 20, 88
Medici, Cosimo de' 11n.
Medici, Giuliano de' xii, xxi, 94, 95n.,
   130
Medici, Lorenzo de' (d. 1492) 3n., 79n.,
   97, 130, 133
Medici, Lorenzo de' (d. 1519) 3, 4, 94n.,
   130
Medici, Piero de' 3n., 43n., 130
Medici family ix, x, xii-xiv, xxi, xxiv, xxvi,
   34, 88–91, 94
Mestre, destruction of 89
Milan ix, xi, 5, 7, 8, 12, 23, 24, 40,
   75–7, 79, 97
Milanese, the 44, 45
Montaigne, Michel de 81n.
Montanari, Fausto 6n.
Montefeltro, Guido Ubaldo xxi, 25n.,
   75, 97, 130–1
Moors, the 77
More, Thomas 81n.
Moses 20, 21, 88, 89n., 105n., 131
Mugello, xxvi

Nabis 36, 64, 131
Nantes 14
Naples, Kingdom of 5, 13, 14, 27, 45,
   77, 86, 88
Navarre 77
Nero xv
Nigrinus 69
Normandy 8
Novara, battle of 7n., 47n.
Numantia 18

Old Testament 50
Oliverotto of Fermo *see* Euffreducci,
   Oliverotto

Cambridge Texts in the History of Political Thought

Titles published in the series thus far

Aristotle *The Politics* and *The Constitution of Athens* (edited by Stephen Everson)
0 521 48400 6 paperback

Arnold *Culture and Anarchy and other writings* (edited by Stefan Collini)
0 521 37796 X paperback

Astell *Political Writings* (edited by Patricia Springborg)
0 521 42845 9 paperback

Augustine *The City of God against the Pagans* (edited by R. W. Dyson)
0 521 46843 4 paperback

Austin *The Province of Jurisprudence Determined* (edited by Wilfrid E. Rumble)
0 521 44756 9 paperback

Bacon *The History of the Reign of King Henry VII* (edited by Brian Vickers)
0 521 58663 1 paperback

Bakunin *Statism and Anarchy* (edited by Marshall Shatz)
0 521 36973 8 paperback

Baxter *Holy Commonwealth* (edited by William Lamont)
0 521 40580 7 paperback

Bayle *Political Writings* (edited by Sally L. Jenkinson)
0 521 47677 1 paperback

Beccaria *On Crimes and Punishments and other writings* (edited by Richard Bellamy)
0 521 47982 7 paperback

Bentham *Fragment on Government* (introduction by Ross Harrison)
0 521 35929 5 paperback

Bernstein *The Preconditions of Socialism* (edited by Henry Tudor)
0 521 39808 8 paperback

Bodin *On Sovereignty* (edited by Julian H. Franklin)
0 521 34992 3 paperback

Bolingbroke *Political Writings* (edited by David Armitage)
0 521 58697 6 paperback

Bossuet *Politics Drawn from the Very Words of Holy Scripture* (edited by Patrick Riley)
0 521 36807 3 paperback

The British Idealists (edited by David Boucher)
0 521 45951 6 paperback

Burke *Pre-Revolutionary Writings* (edited by Ian Harris)
0 521 36800 6 paperback

Christine De Pizan *The Book of the Body Politic* (edited by Kate Langdon Forhan)
0 521 42259 0 paperback

Cicero *On Duties* (edited by M. T. Griffin and E. M. Atkins)
0 521 34835 8 paperback

Cicero *On the Commonwealth and On the Laws* (edited by James E. G. Zetzel)
0 521 45959 1 paperback

Comte *Early Political Writings* (edited by H. S. Jones)
  0 521 46923 6 paperback
Conciliarism and Papalism (edited by J. H. Burns and Thomas M. Izbicki)
  0 521 47674 7 paperback
Constant *Political Writings* (edited by Biancamaria Fontana)
  0 521 31632 4 paperback
Dante *Monarchy* (edited by Prue Shaw)
  0 521 56781 5 paperback
Diderot *Political Writings* (edited by John Hope Mason and Robert Wokler)
  0 521 36911 8 paperback
The Dutch Revolt (edited by Martin van Gelderen)
  0 521 39809 6 paperback
Early Greek Political Thought from Homer to the Sophists (edited by Michael Gagarin
  and Paul Woodruff)
  0 521 43768 7 paperback
The Early Political Writings of the German Romantics (edited by
  Frederick C. Beiser)
  0 521 44951 0 paperback
The English Levellers (edited by Andrew Sharp)
  0 521 62511 4 paperback
Erasmus *The Education of a Christian Prince* (edited by Lisa Jardine)
  0 521 58811 1 paperback
Fenelon *Telemachus* (edited by Patrick Riley)
  0 521 45662 2 paperback
Ferguson *An Essay on the History of Civil Society* (edited by Fania Oz-Salzberger)
  0 521 44736 4 paperback
Filmer *Patriarcha and Other Writings* (edited by Johann P. Sommerville)
  0 521 39903 3 paperback
Fletcher *Political Works* (edited by John Robertson)
  0 521 43994 9 paperback
Sir John Fortescue *On the Laws and Governance of England* (edited by
  Shelley Lockwood)
  0 521 58996 7 paperback
Fourier *The Theory of the Four Movements* (edited by Gareth Stedman Jones and Ian
  Patterson)
  0 521 35693 8 paperback
Gramsci *Pre-Prison Writings* (edited by Richard Bellamy)
  0 521 42307 4 paperback
Guicciardini *Dialogue on the Government of Florence* (edited by Alison Brown)
  0 521 45623 1 paperback
Harrington *A Commonwealth of Oceana* and *A System of Politics* (edited by
  J. G. A. Pocock)
  0 521 42329 5 paperback

Hegel *Elements of the Philosophy of Right* (edited by Allen W. Wood and
H. B. Nisbet)
0 521 34888 9 paperback
Hegel *Political Writings* (edited by Laurence Dickey and H. B. Nisbet)
0 521 45979 3 paperback
Hobbes *On the Citizen* (edited by Michael Silverthorne and Richard Tuck)
0 521 43780 6 paperback
Hobbes *Leviathan* (edited by Richard Tuck)
0 521 56797 1 paperback
Hobhouse *Liberalism and Other Writings* (edited by James Meadowcroft)
0 521 43726 1 paperback
Hooker *Of the Laws of Ecclesiastical Polity* (edited by A. S. McGrade)
0 521 37908 3 paperback
Hume *Political Essays* (edited by Knud Haakonssen)
0 521 46639 3 paperback
King James VI and I *Political Writings* (edited by Johann P. Sommerville)
0 521 44729 1 paperback
Jefferson *Political Writings* (edited by Joyce Appleby and Terence Ball)
0 521 64841 6 paperback
John of Salisbury *Policraticus* (edited by Cary Nederman)
0 521 36701 8 paperback
Kant *Political Writings* (edited by H. S. Reiss and H. B. Nisbet)
0 521 39837 1 paperback
Knox *On Rebellion* (edited by Roger A. Mason)
0 521 39988 2 paperback
Kropotkin *The Conquest of Bread and other writings* (edited by Marshall Shatz)
0 521 45990 7 paperback
Lawson *Politica sacra et civilis* (edited by Conal Condren)
0 521 39248 9 paperback
Leibniz *Political Writings* (edited by Patrick Riley)
0 521 35899 X paperback
The Levellers (edited by Andrew Sharp)
0 521 62511 4 paperback
Locke *Political Essays* (edited by Mark Goldie)
0 521 47861 8 paperback
Locke *Two Treatises of Government* (edited by Peter Laslett)
0 521 35730 6 paperback
Loyseau *A Treatise of Orders and Plain Dignities* (edited by Howell A. Lloyd)
0 521 45624 X paperback
Luther and Calvin on Secular Authority (edited by Harro Höpfl)
0 521 34986 9 paperback
Machiavelli *The Prince* (edited by Quentin Skinner and Russell Price)
0 521 34993 1 paperback

de Maistre *Considerations on France* (edited by Isaiah Berlin and Richard Lebrun)
0 521 46628 8 paperback
Malthus *An Essay on the Principle of Population* (edited by Donald Winch)
0 521 42972 2 paperback
Marsiglio of Padua *Defensor minor* and *De translatione Imperii* (edited by
Cary Nederman)
0 521 40846 6 paperback
Marx *Early Political Writings* (edited by Joseph O'Malley)
0 521 34994 X paperback
Marx *Later Political Writings* (edited by Terrell Carver)
0 521 36739 5 paperback
James Mill *Political Writings* (edited by Terence Ball)
0 521 38748 5 paperback
J. S. Mill *On Liberty*, with *The Subjection of Women* and *Chapters on Socialism* (edited
by Stefan Collini)
0 521 37917 2 paperback
Milton *Political Writings* (edited by Martin Dzelzainis)
0 521 34866 8 paperback
Montesquieu *The Spirit of the Laws* (edited by Anne M. Cohler, Basia Carolyn Miller
and Harold Samuel Stone)
0 521 36974 6 paperback
More *Utopia* (edited by George M. Logan and Robert M. Adams)
0 521 40318 9 paperback
Morris *News from Nowhere* (edited by Krishan Kumar)
0 521 42233 7 paperback
Nicholas of Cusa *The Catholic Concordance* (edited by Paul E. Sigmund)
0 521 56773 4 paperback
Nietzsche *On the Genealogy of Morality* (edited by Keith Ansell-Pearson)
0 521 40610 2 paperback
Paine *Political Writings* (edited by Bruce Kuklick)
0 521 36678 X paperback
Plato *Statesman* (edited by Julia Annas and Robin Waterfield)
0 521 44778 X paperback
Price *Political Writings* (edited by D. O. Thomas)
0 521 40969 1 paperback
Priestley *Political Writings* (edited by Peter Miller)
0 521 42561 1 paperback
Proudhon *What is Property?* (edited by Donald R. Kelley and
Bonnie G. Smith)
0 521 40556 4 paperback
Pufendorf *On the Duty of Man and Citizen according to Natural Law* (edited by James
Tully)
0 521 35980 5 paperback

The Radical Reformation (edited by Michael G. Baylor)

   0 521 37948 2 paperback

Rousseau *The Discourses and other early political writings* (edited by
Victor Gourevitch)

   0 521 42445 3 paperback

Rousseau *The Social Contract and other later political writings* (edited by
Victor Gourevitch)

   0 521 42446 1 paperback

Seneca *Moral and Political Essays* (edited by John Cooper and John Procope)

   0 521 34818 8 paperback

Sidney *Court Maxims* (edited by Hans W. Blom, Eco Haitsma Mulier and
Ronald Janse)

   0 521 46736 5 paperback

Sorel *Reflections on Violence* (edited by Jeremy Jennings)

   0 521 55910 3 paperback

Spencer *The Man versus the State* and *The Proper Sphere of Government*
(edited by John Offer)

   0 521 43740 7 paperback

Stirner *The Ego and Its Own* (edited by David Leopold)

   0 521 45647 9 paperback

Thoreau *Political Writings* (edited by Nancy Rosenblum)

   0 521 47675 5 paperback

Utopias of the British Enlightenment (edited by Gregory Claeys)

   0 521 45590 1 paperback

Vitoria *Political Writings* (edited by Anthony Pagden and Jeremy Lawrance)

   0 521 36714 X paperback

Voltaire *Political Writings* (edited by David Williams)

   0 521 43727 X paperback

Weber *Political Writings* (edited by Peter Lassman and Ronald Speirs)

   0 521 39719 7 paperback

William of Ockham *A Short Discourse on Tyrannical Government* (edited by
A. S. McGrade and John Kilcullen)

   0 521 35803 5 paperback

William of Ockham *A Letter to the Friars Minor and other writings* (edited by
A. S. McGrade and John Kilcullen)

   0 521 35804 3 paperback

Wollstonecraft *A Vindication of the Rights of Men* and *A Vindication of the Rights of
Woman* (edited by Sylvana Tomaselli)

   0 521 43633 8 paperback